THE ESSENCE OF
STABILITY BALL TRAINING:

COMPANION GUIDE

By

Juan Carlos Santana

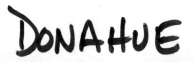

ISBN 0-9708116-0-8

For information contact:
Juan Carlos Santana, MEd, CSCS
Optimum Performance Systems
438 NW 13 St
Boca Raton, Florida, 33432
(561) 393-3881

Video Captures by
Greg Sammons

Special Contributors and Editors
Diane Vives, BSE, CSCS
Gary Lavin, BSE, CSCS

Patricia Cinao, Editorial Assistant

Published by
Optimum Performance Systems
Boca Raton, Florida

About the Author

Juan Carlos "JC" Santana is an international authority on performance enhancement and is one of the most sought after and prolific speakers in the fitness industry. JC has published extensively and produced many videos on the subject of performance enhancement. His educational resources bring the most innovative and cutting edge training methodology to fitness professionals around the world.

JC received his BS and MEd degrees in Exercise Science from Florida Atlantic University, where he also served as an adjunct professor of Weight Training Systems and Sports Training Systems. He is currently a pursuing his doctorate degree from the University of Miami.

JC is a member and a certified Health Fitness Instructor with the ACSM, and a member and Certified Strength and Conditioning Specialist (CSCS) with the National Strength and Conditioning Association (NSCA). He is a certified Senior Coach and Club Coach Course Instructor with the USAWF, and a LEVEL I coach with the US Track and Field Association. Currently, Carlos serves as the Chairman for the NSCA's Sport Specific Conference, a NSCA Conference Committee member and is the NSCA's Florida State Director.

JC has directed and operated several fitness facilities in the Miami, Hollywood and Boca Raton areas. He is now the Director of the "Functional Integrated Training (F.I.T). Institute" in Boca Raton Florida, a state-of-the-art training facility servicing a clientele that ranges from elite athletes to the neurologically challenged. JC is the director of his consulting company, Optimum Performance Systems (OPS), which is based out of the FIT Institute. OPS provides: Consulting for equipment manufactures, fitness organizations, fitness professionals and major sports teams, athletic development camps, education for fitness professionals and internships for graduates in the allied health professions.

Acknowledgement

I would like to take a brief moment to acknowledge and thank all of my predecessors who have advanced the development of the stability ball as a performance-enhancement tool. A special acknowledgement to the work of Aquilliono Cosani, Dr. Elsbeth Kong, Dr. Susan Klien-Vogelbach, Maria Kucera-Locher, Mary Quinton, Beate Carrriere, Kathie Hanson, Liz Schorn, Joanne Posner-Mayer, Elizabeth Noble, Ilana Parker, Dr. Ninoska Gomez, Barbara Hypes, Caroline Creager, Paul Calloway, Paul Check and all the dedicated therapists, trainers and coaches that have advanced the competencies of the "performance enhancement" profession.

Although their names are too many to mention, a few friends and colleagues have pioneered performance enhancement techniques and methodology, and have been particularly influential in my professional and personal development. This work is also theirs!

Many thanks to:

*My colleagues, professors and all of the interns from Florida Atlantic University and University of Miami Exercise Science and Physiology programs. A special thanks to my Ph.D. advisor, Dr. Joe Signorile, for keeping the "flame of knowledge" burning bright within me.

*Gary Gray, Vern Gambetta and Mike Clark for teaching me to ask "why" and opening the doors to the concept of "function" and, most of all, for the "Parakletos".

*Drs. A. Abbott, J. Antonio, T. Bompa, J. Chandler, S. Fleck, W. Fry, W. Kraemer, R. Kreider, R. Newton, P. Roetert, and Mike Stone for advancing our field and always willing to answer my questions.

*Mike Burgener, Rafael Guerrero and Leo Totten for their inspiration and insight into explosive lifting, and teaching me what "raw power" is all about.

*My friends and professional associates Mike Ashley, Bill Hebson, Tom Incledon, Greg and Edie Sammons, for making our past and future collaborations what they should be – exciting adventures!

*MF Athletic and all the supporters of our seminar series in South Florida for their support and encouragement.

Special thanks to:
Diane Vives and Gary Lavin
For their loyalty, friendship and professionalism.
OPS would not be where it is today without you!

Finally, "Mi Familia",
For nurturing a life of principles
and fueling the "will to power".
My heart and love remain forever yours!

La Familia:
Debbie, Rio and Caila Santana
Arnaldo and Celerina Santana
Lee, Belkis, Eric, and the undying spirit of Rick Olson
Javier, Monica, Stephonie, and Madison Machado
Donald Jones   -JCS

Table of Content

Purpose of Book

This book is best suited to accompany the Essence of Stability Ball Training (ESBT), Volumes I and II. Although the ESBT video series is the most comprehensive stability ball (SB) project in the fitness industry, it is impossible to bring extensive detailed information through the medium of video without multiple volumes. Thus, this book covers much detailed information, which compliments the visual information of the video series.

Other publications have attempted to address the various uses and applications of the SB. However, most have been clinically oriented and tailored to therapist and clinicians. Therefore, it is the purpose of this book to provide a comprehensive "hands on" approach to stability ball training for the conditioning specialist and personal trainer. This text will cover the following major topics:

- ✓ History and evolution of the SB
- ✓ Rational and science behind SB training
- ✓ Basic functional anatomy of the body's core musculature
- ✓ SB training methodology
- ✓ SB training application and programming
- ✓ Integration into traditional strength training programs
- ✓ Sample programs
- ✓ Recommended readings

Much of the information we will present has come about through bold exploration and creative implementation by our predecessors in this area of conditioning. As they were intrinsically inspired to take a "toy" and adopt it into a clinical environment, this text aims to inspire the reader to always look for the "diamond in the rough". The next "stability ball" could be right under your nose.

Tradition is based many times on success. However, much of this tradition is based on "clinically-unexamined, passed-down" information. The typical "that's the way it's always been" rationale. In order to separate fact from fiction, one must always be willing to ask the "why" of tradition. Therefore, a secondary purpose of this book is to stimulate critical thinking. The type of thinking that invokes curiosity and exploration of possibilities – the thinking that leads to the constant examination of traditional training principles.

This book will also introduce a concept of training we have coined as "Stabilization Limited Training" (SLT). This type of training is characterized by limiting prime mover force production, by the strength of the stabilizing structures. SLT was developed like most training concepts we use today. It was first successfully utilized, then described.

Strength and conditioning leaders often propose many innovative training ideas and professional journals constantly provide a plethora of ingenious training modalities. However, most of the thrust behind articles remains the introduction and description of the training modality, not its integration into a traditional training program. This book will provide a comprehensive approach to Stability Ball (SB) Training, as well as an integration model. Extensive examples of protocols and their place within traditional training models will also be provided within this series.

A Brief History of the Stability Ball

One of the most versatile pieces of equipment used today by conditioning professionals is the SB (i.e. "Swiss balls", "Fit-balls", Physioballs", etc.). The SB has had long-standing success in the world of clinical rehabilitation. However, due to their effectiveness in developing balance and core strength, we now see athletic trainers, coaches, personal trainers and physical education teachers integrating them into their programs. The SB has definitely emerged as a new craze in the world of athletic and functional conditioning.

The history of the SB originates back to the early 1960s. It was made by an Italian toy maker, Aquilino Cosani, and sold primarily in Europe as the Gymnastik. In 1981 Cosani started a new company, Gymnic. These two companies are still active in Italy and are the major suppliers of SBs throughout the world.

The SB's clinical application by Dr. Susan Klein-Vogelbach, a Swiss PT, can be traced back to the 1960s. Through a series of classes, seminars and clinical workshops, the SB made its way to the San Francisco area in the 1980s. Since the 1980s, the SB has slowly gone from the rehabilitation setting into the fitness and athletic arena. Paul Chek, NMT, was one of the pioneers in the evolution of the stability ball as a performance enhancement tool. In the late 1980s, he was one of the first to use the SB to rehabilitate and condition athletes. Due to the SB's success and growing popularity, the last decade has seen the birth of various programs developed to educate professionals on their use.

In Europe, SBs have been used in schools as chairs. The benefit of this type of application has been reported as improved focus, handwriting skills, better understanding of class material and better organizational skills. There are several pilot studies in the US using the SB in school settings. The preliminary reports are consistent with those found in Europe.

A note on history and originality

All of the modern training methods are mere recreations of training methods used by our predecessors. The body only moves in so many ways, therefore, there is little that anyone can come up with that has not been done before. Look at all of the "new functional modalities," like the stability ball, and you will see that mankind has "been there and done that." Even animals have previously accomplished what some fitness professionals claim to have invented. Just because one has an original thought does not mean one was the first to think it!

The use of ball balancing can be traced back to the circus and theatre. Acrobats and clowns have been using balls as part of their acts for many years. Still today, many acts are still performed on balls. We are currently working with the Circus World Museum to obtain a brief history and any pictures that may be available on the use of ball balance. The following page illustrates a few pictures they have provided.

These wonderful drawings were provided by Erin Foley, of the Circus World Museum, and are from the 1800s. According to Erin, "the rolling globes and cylinders would have been used earlier in theatrical performance than in the circus due to the flat surface they required. Circuses were usually performed under tents and uneven ground."

Diversity of settings, populations and applications

Once limited to the rehabilitation and clinical setting, the SB has permeated to all sectors of the health and fitness community. In clinics, they are still used to provide a gentle proprioceptive stimuli for individuals recovering from surgery. John Leonard is one of Florida's finest PTs. He says, "we have found the SB to be our most versatile piece of equipment. It's fun, it's colorful and everybody from our pediatric patients to our geriatric patients literally find the SB to be something unique and that they can generate some enthusiasm about. The uniqueness about the SB is that it utilizes the neuromuscular system in a way that no other exercise equipment, I have come across has. That is, it incorporates the use of:
- multiple muscle systems
- neurologically induced muscular responses
- the body's own normal processes to establish and restore balance."

From the clinical setting, the SB made its way to the sports arena in the 1990s. Therapists with athletic backgrounds realized that the SB could be applied more aggressively to actually enhance the performance of athletes. Now, the SB can be found in just about every professional strength facility. Articles that include many high profile athletes using the SB have made their way into conditioning magazines, furthering the SB's acceptance.

As the popularity of the SB grew, it also started to make its way into fitness conferences. As professionals delivered educational presentations, personal trainers immediately saw it as a tool to enhance client interest and performance. Personal trainers have now introduced the SBs into commercial training facilities. Soon SB articles appeared in popular fitness magazines at an increasing rate, creating the increased awareness we see today. Just about every commercial gym I to now has at least one SB. Some gyms have even developed group classes that incorporate the SB with other equipment, such as barbells and medicine balls.

JC presented the largest SB workshop in fitness history. In Nov. 2000, over 350 attendees participated in this historic event at the UBC. Thanks to the Bird Coop staff – the impossible became an exciting reality!

Due to the stability ball's popularity within the rehabilitation and fitness industry, they have made their way into the private sector. Although the initial home use might have been rehabilitation, the stability ball is now used by many as a chair for their office, for regular strength training, and for play. Most, if not all, of my clients have them at home and regularly utilize them to keep their core functioning at its optimum. My clients also report that anyone who comes into a room and sees the SB, ends up asking questions about the SB, as they sit and begin to play on it. They are "a natural" for fun and play – what better training tool?

JC presenting a workshop on the SB. MF hosted this seminar at the Reggie Lewis center in Boston. Four groups of 75 attendees, ranging from professional coaches to personal trainers, rotated for an entire day and loved the concept of the SB.

JC presents to smaller private groups in Chicago. Phenomenal Fitness was the site of this friendly and energetic seminar. Personal trainers, coaches and rehab specialists were among the attendees.

The Science and Practice of SB Training

The effectiveness of the SB can be partially gauged by its increasing popularity and reported results. However, not all fitness professionals agree on the efficacy of its use. One of the issues that opponents of SB training always address is the lack of "specific" scientific research on stability ball training. Although specific research on the SB is practically impossible to find at this time, there is abundant science that implicitly substantiates the efficacy of its use. When reviewing the spine and trunk stabilization work completed by Saal, Grabiner, Robinson, Hodges, Liebenson & Hyman and others, their hypothesis implicitly confirm the use of SB in spine rehabilitation and athletic conditioning.

When viewing the anatomy of the spine, one of the most interesting observations is the deep segmental muscles involved in stabilization. These segmental muscles, such as the multifidus, play a very important role during the stabilization of the spine and functional movements. Coaches and trainers use exercises such as deadlifts, goodmornings, or squats, to strengthen the spine. Yet, these traditional methods of strengthening the spine have not been effective in developing these very important spinal stabilizers.

The isometric lordotic position used in Goodmornings does not allow optimal recruitment of the intersegmental spinal musculature.

Although these exercises are effective for strengthening the hips and spinal erectors, the lordotic posture used during the execution of these lifts does not provide the ultimate stimuli for their development. The SB can provide a training environment where gentle flexion and extension of the spine can be trained. This allows the multi-segmental musculature to be fully engaged and trained. Consequently, the development of these spinal muscles allows better postural control and the potential for greater efficiency in movement.

Notice the flexed spine supported at the beginning of the hyperextension

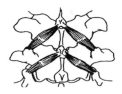
Rotatores

Interspinales

Intertransversarii

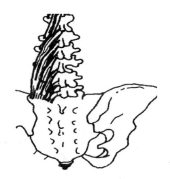

Due to the positioning of these muscles, these muscles do not see significant work in isometric lordotic positions. Lighter flexion extension exercises are more effective for targeting this musculature.

Multifidus

Reproduced with permission of K.W. Sieg and S.P. Adams (1996) <u>Illustrated Essentials of Musculoskeletal Anatomy</u>, Megabooks, Inc. Gainsville, Fl. Pages 149, 150.

Symmetry of movement has also been identified in the literature as a every important aspect of spinal stabilization. Studies by Grabiner have indicated that strength alone does not necessarily correlate with normal function. Subjects with lower back pain (LBP) have consistently shown a lack of symmetry in paraspinal contraction during trunk extension. This lack of neuromuscular symmetry has been able to predict LBP in subjects who have been tested normal on dynamometry. Many SB exercises require symmetrical contraction of the paraspinals for successful exercise execution. Asymmetrical contractions will cause the body to lose balance and roll off the SB. Balancing on the SB may require asymmetrical contractions, but they must be deliberate and controlled in order to maintain balance on the SB.

The scientific literature may not be very explicit in its endorsement of SB training in spinal stabilization and performance enhancement. However, it does not take a rocket scientist to realize that an individual with a functional spine will move better and be less likely to suffer an injury. We have seen my clients improve their 1-3RM squatting and lunging ability by as much as 50%, without doing heavy squats, lunges or leg presses. We credit much of their improvement to the core stabilization work we perform using various modalities, including the SB.

There is also a significant body of work demonstrating the importance of the deep abdominal musculature in providing trunk stabilization, particularly the transverse abdominals and obliques. Many of the studies show that movement, specifically stabilization, originates from the core of the body. Many of the models have demonstrated in healthy subjects the deep abdominal musculature (i.e. the transverse abdominals) will contract prior to the extremities, during reactions to postural perturbations. This sequential and preferential recruitment begins to shed some light on the importance of this muscle group in providing core stability.

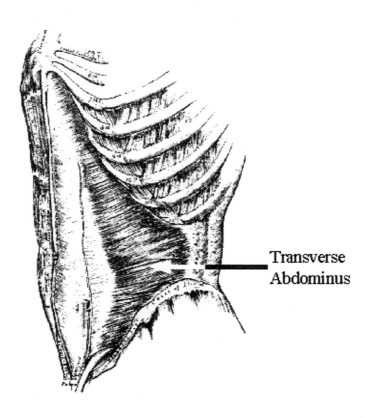

Notice the orientation of the fibers in the abdominal musculature. The transverse abdominus is the only one that has a horizontal orientation. Therefore, it is the muscle that has the best position to create the same support as a weight lifting belt (i.e. support the spine by increasing inter-abdominal pressure). The concomitant contracture of the internal and external obliques will also provide additional horizontal stabilization mechanism.

The works by Nachemson, Saal, Wirhed, Hodges, and others, describe the enormous loads on the spine during daily activities, and the roll the abdominal muscles play in stabilizing the spine during these activities. They all conclude that abdominal training is the cornerstone of any core stabilization program. This body of the research advocates isometric, dynamic and unstable training to develop the deep muscles of the abdominals involved in core stability. The stability ball allows one to implement a variety of exercises that require isometric stabilization and even explosive contractions geared to activate the fast twitch fibers. The SB's unstable nature also provides perturbation stimulus, which has been shown to help preferentially recruit the deep abdominal musculature. Additionally, due to the SB's ability to roll in any direction, it provides training stimuli in all three planes of motion.

Another area of research that may add some insight into the efficacy of SB training is that of vibration research. Vibratory stimuli has been shown to have an impact on force production, as well as induce various tissue changes. The work by Bosco and

Necking has shown that vibration training can increase power and induce hypertrophy. . The exact mechanisms for these adaptations are still unexplained by researchers. Although these vibration studies are specific to precise and constant frequencies that cannot be exactly simulated on the SB, the vibration induced by the instability of the SB cannot be automatically ruled ineffective. Additionally, the 5 sets of 90-120 second dose used in vibration studies is not out of the realm of a one hour workout session partially using the SB. The duration of Bosco's research was 10 days. Coincidentally, this is about the time when we start to see major improvements in stability and strength in our clients, athletes and non-athletes.

The unstable nature of SB training, creates a vibratory-like stimulus. It is hard to tell whether this vibration stimuli works in a similar fashion, as the vibration protocols used in Bosco's and Necking's research.

The unstable quality of the SB has an impact on the neutralizers and stabilizers of any joint involved in a movement. For example, the stabilization required to maintain a push-up position (i.e. hands on the ball feet on the floor), recruits and develops the stabilizers and neutralizers of the shoulder girdle/joint in a way that a chest machine cannot. The improved joint function, due to this stabilization work, results in increased joint integrity, decreased injury potential and increased efficiency in force production. We have also seen as much as 40-50% improvement in our client's bench presses with little bench work. Most of our athletes do very little benching, yet they attain respectable 1RMs and continuously improve their PRs. We accredit this again to the stabilization work we do on the SB and other functional modalities. More importantly, we see little in the way of overuse injuries resulting from pattern overloads associated with stabilized strength training modalities.

A popular concern expressed to me by many fitness professionals is the involvement of the CNS. Many conditioning specialist are concerned that this form of training really taxes the CNS and this can lead to overtraining, neurologically or morphologically. Although this may happen at the beginning stages of training, this training has never resulted in overtraining in our facility. We believe the reasons for this are multi-factorial.

First, due to the stabilization demands, the prime movers never get an enormous isolated stimulus, so they don't have the chance to reach an overtraining stage. Second, due to the unstable training environment of the SB, the path of motion is never the same. Therefore, the neural pattern overload we often see in machine-based training is never seen in SB training. Third, SB training is skill dominant – it's highly neural. That means the adaptations occur extremely fast, sometimes within a single session. This is consistent with what we know about strength training. We know that the initial strength gains at the beginning stages of training are mostly due to neural adaptation. Therefore, what is neurally taxing today, is a warm-up a few weeks later. It's just like learning how to ride a bike or skipping rope – very hard at first, but soon it becomes automatic and non-challenging. With these factors in mind, don't be afraid of over training the CNS. Like the muscular system, it also adapts. The skills involved in SB training are also learned at an alarming rate and soon become automatic and yours forever – even with little training. Just use proper progression and everything else works out.

In conclusion, the research on SB's is not specific to its use. Rather, it describes beneficial training mechanisms targeted by it use. It is the responsibility of the conditioning professional to read through the scientific literature and extrapolate the knowledge it imparts. Then, apply training principles that are based on, but perhaps not explicitly described by, science and tested by time. Most successful training principles are not initially described by science anyway. They are developed and described by practitioners – science merely substantiates their efficacy many years after the fact. Therefore, beware of an overemphasis on the need for explicit scientific research – a lifetime may pass you by. Effective training methodology usually "feels" right and more important "makes sense." The optimal criteria I try to strive for, when developing and implementing our training programs, is:

1) Have a strong basis in science; not necessarily described by it
2) Have a history substantiating its efficacy (i.e. be field tested)
3) Make sense
4) Be "doable"
5) Be fun.

Being results oriented, I personally don't get too caught up in what came first "the chicken or the egg." Consequently, I do not put too much emphasis on whether "science explained it before the practitioner utilized it effectively." Results are results and speak for themselves.

Basic anatomy of the body's core

In order to properly train the body's core a basic understanding of its musculature and function are essential. To that end, this section will provide some basic information on the muscles of the core and their function. In no way is this section meant to be a comprehensive review of the core's anatomy or its function. For an extensive review of this topic, we strongly recommend the educational resources provided by Mike Clark and Gary Gray.

Spinal Stabilization

The main function of the core is to stabilize the spine in response to balance perturbations and connecting the hips to the shoulders during force production. Although stabilization is the most commonly mentioned function of the core, explosive force production is one of its most utilized functions. This is especially true in the transverse plane. Multi planar rotation is perhaps the most neglected training stimulus.

The following are some of the major muscle structures of the core. We encourage the reader to use these illustrations for quick reference and further reading of a more advanced and detailed nature.

a) Abdominals (refer to previous chapter for larger images)
(B) = bilateral   (U) = unilateral   (I) = integrated

≈ **Rectus Abdominus**
(B) – Flexes trunk and increases intra-abdominal pressure.
(U)- ipsilateral flexion.
(I)- Eccentrically decelerates trunk extension, lateral flexion and rotation. Also decelerates anterior pelvic tilt.

≈ **External Obliques**
(B) - Trunk Flexion
(U)- Lateral flex and contralateral rot.
(I) – Eccentrically decelerates trunk extension, lateral flexion, and rotation. Also, works as an integrated functional unit in the transverse plane force couple mechanism.

≈ **Internal Obliques**
(B) – Trunk Flex
(U) – Lateral flex and ipsilateral rot.
(I) – Eccentrically decelerates extension, rotation, and lateral flexion. Works synergistically with the Transverse Abdominus to provide rotational and translational stability to the lumbar spine

≈ **Transverse Abdominus**
(B) – Increases intra-abdominal pressure.
(I)- As a Feed-Forward Mechanism, it works to preferentially stabilize the lumbar spine. Also, it synergistically works with the Internal Oblique, Multifidus, and Deep Erector Spinae to stabilize lumbo-pelvic-hip complex.

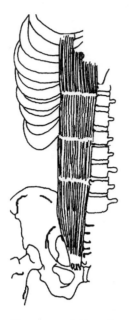

Rectus abdominus

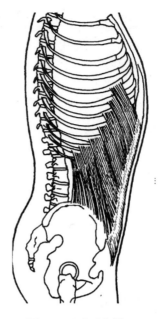

External Obliques

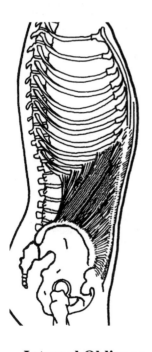

Internal Obliques

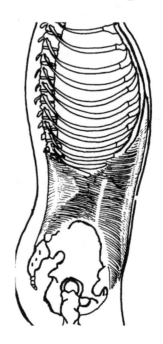

Transverse abdominus

Reproduced with permission of K.W. Sieg and S.P. Adams (1996) <u>Illustrated Essentials of Musculoskeletal Anatomy</u>, Megabooks, Inc. Gainsville, Fl. Pages 139-142.

b)   Paraspinals and Latissimus

≈   **Quadratus Lumborum**

(B) – Spinal ext.

(U)- Lateral flex.

(I) – Works synergistically with the Gluteus Medius, Tensor Fascia, and Adductor Complex as the primary frontal plane stabilization mechanism.

≈   **Multifidus**

(B) – Spinal ext.

(U)- Rotation to opposite side

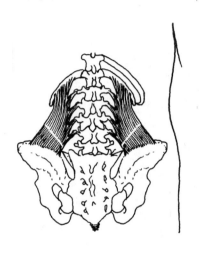

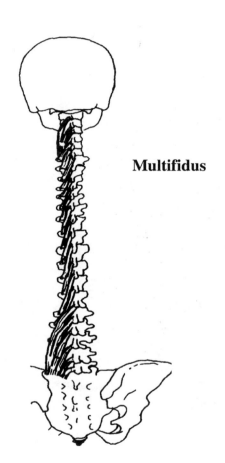

Multifidus

Quadratus Lumborum

Reproduced with permission of K.W. Sieg and S.P. Adams (1996) Illustrated Essentials of Musculoskeletal Anatomy, Megabooks, Inc. Gainsville, Fl. Pages 146, 149.

≈ **Erector Spinae Group**.
- **Spinalis**- (B)-Spinal ext., (U)-ipsilateral flexion.
- **Longissimus** – (B) – Ext., of spine, (U) – Ipsilateral flexion of the spine.
- **Iliocostalis** –(B)- Ext. of spine, (U) – Ipsilateral side flexion.
(I)- Together, these muscles eccentrically decelerate flexion, rotation, and lateral flexion, as well as dynamically stabilizes the spine during functional movements.

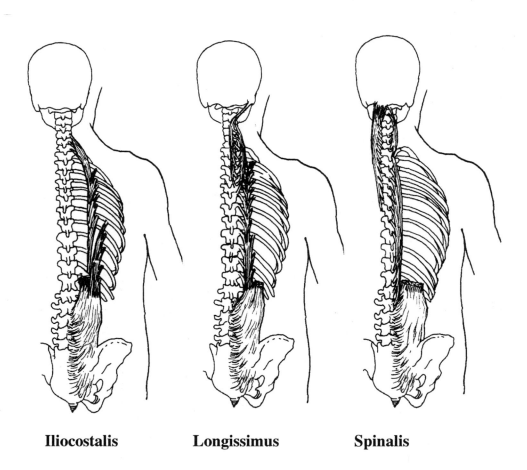

Iliocostalis   **Longissimus**   **Spinalis**

Reproduced with permission of K.W. Sieg and S.P. Adams (1996) <u>*Illustrated Essentials of Musculoskeletal Anatomy*</u>, *Megabooks, Inc. Gainsville, Fl. Page 148.*

≈ **Latissimus Dorsi** –
(B)- Extension
(U) - Medial rotation and adduction of humerus
(I) - Accelerates Internal rotation of the arm and provides stability to the hip complex.

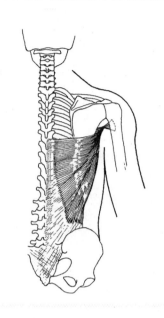

Latissimus Dorsi

≈ **Transversospinalis**
- **Rotatores** – extension of spine and rotation to opposite side.
- **Interspinales** – extension of spine.
- **Intertransversarri** – lateral flexion of spine.

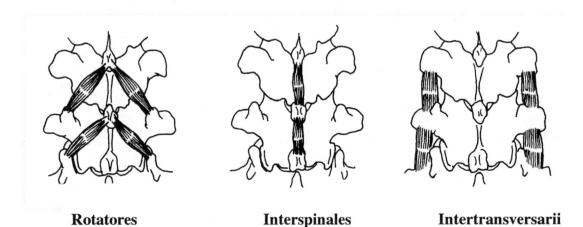

Rotatores   **Interspinales**   **Intertransversarii**

c)   **Major Hip Extensors and Abductors**
  1.   **Gluteus Maximus** – Extension of hip, external rotation of the hip and adduction (lower fibers).
  2.   **Gluteus Medius** - Abduction of hip, external/internal rotation of hip as it abducts.
  3.   **Gluteus Minimus** – Abduction of hip, internal rotation of hip as it abducts.
  4.   **Biceps Femoris** – Extension of the hip, flexion of the knee, external rotation of the hip, external rotation of the knee.
  5.   **A-Semitendinosus and b-semimebranosus** – Extension and internal rotation of the hip, internal rotation of the knee
  6.   **Tensor fasciae latae-** Flexion, abduction, and internal rotation of the femur
  7.   **Iliopsoas-** Flexes hip, abduction and lateral rotation of the hip
  8.   **Sartorius-** abducts the hip and externally rotates the femur.

Integrated functions of the hip extensors and abductors
– Eccentrically decelerates femoral adduction during swing phase
– Eccentrically decelerates hip flexion and leg extension prior to heel strike
– Eccentrically decelerates hip flexion at heel strike
– Eccentrically decelerates femoral adduction and tibial internal rotation at mid-stance and during lateral changes in direction
– Accelerates hip extension, external rotation and abduction prior to heel strike
– Accelerates hip extension and external rotation during push-off and lateral changes of direction

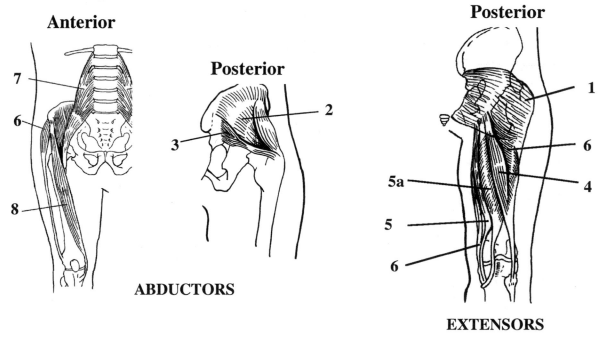

Reproduced with permission of K.W. Sieg and S.P. Adams (1996) <u>Illustrated Essentials of Musculoskeletal Anatomy</u>, Megabooks, Inc. Gainsville, Fl. Pages 120-121.

Hip Flexors and adductors

1. **Iliopsoas** –Hip flexion, external rotation of the femur. May also flex (B) and rotate (U) trunk to opposite side when extremity is fixed (closed chain).
2. **Pectineus** – Hip flexion, adduction and internal rotation of the hip.
3. **Tensor Fascia Latae** – Hip flexion, and hip abduction
4. **Adductor brevis** – Adducts, flexes and internally rotates the femur.
5. **Adductor longus** – Adducts, flexes and internally rotates the femur.
6. **Adductor magnus** - Adducts, flexes and internally rotates the femur.
7. **Rectus femoris** - Hip flexion, knee extension (open chain).
8. **Sartorius** - Hip flexion, external rotation of femur and knee flexion (open chain).
9. **Gracilis** – Adducts, flexes, and internally rotates the femur

Integrated Function of the hip flexors and adductors-

- Eccentrically decelerates femoral abduction at top of swing phase and prior to heel strike
- Eccentrically decelerates femoral internal rotation at heel strike
- Eccentrically decelerates hip extension, abduction and external rotation during triple extension
- Eccentrically decelerates knee flexion at heel strike
- Dynamically stabilizes the hip in the frontal plane at midstance
- Accelerates adduction at the end of push-off phase
- Accelerates hip flexion and adduction during swing phase

Anterior

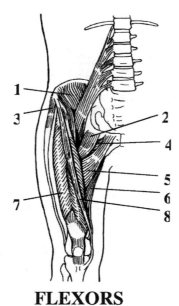

FLEXORS

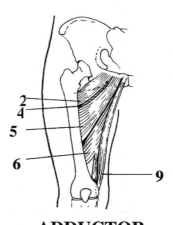

ADDUCTOR

Reproduced with permission of K.W. Sieg and S.P. Adams (1996) Illustrated Essentials of Musculoskeletal Anatomy, Megabooks, Inc. Gainsville, Fl. Pages 120-121.

Stabilization Limited Training ("SLT")

SLT is a term we coined to describe the type of functional strength training that limits force production to the strength and balance of the stabilizing structures (i.e. primarily the core and peripheral joints), not the isolated force capabilities of the prime movers. This has been called "functional training" by various conditioning specialists. However, I believe there is a slight theoretical difference between functional training and SLT. In order to maintain clarity and continuity, let's take a moment to provide some operational definitions for terms we will use.

≈ **Function** – A utility or purpose. "A specific outcome a thing/activity is intended for."

≈ **Functional movement** can be defined as, "a movement with a specific purpose (e.g. skill, or action) as a final outcome." Most human movement is integrated and multi-planar in nature. It also deals with the physical elements of our operational environment (i.e. gravity, momentum, inertia, and impulse).

≈ **Functional Training** can be simply defined as, "a comprehensive training approach that aims to enhance the performance parameters of a specific movement, or target activity." The movement patterns of the training will closely mimic the activity targeted for improvement. However, this is not always the case. Functional training, like most things, is a spectrum! There is no distinct line, or criteria, that separates functional, somewhat functional, non-functional or dysfunctional training (is there such a thing?). Remember, "functional" is a spectrum and what is functional to one application is not functional to another (e.g. a preacher curl is very functional to a bodybuilder, but not to a swimmer).

≈ **SLT** is one of many functional training methods used to enhance performance. It is under the "comprehensive training approach" umbrella. Its focus is on structural stabilization and strength, rather than prime mover isolation or bio-motor skill acquisition. You could make an argument that most of, if not all, of functional training is SLT to some degree. The main difference between the two would be that functional training would have greater specificity of movement to the target activity, thus, greater biomotor skill acquisition. But, that is "beer and peanuts" conversation.

4 Hip lifts supported on ball of one foot

Here is an example of a very effective exercise for runners. Although the movement does not appear to be specific to running on first sight, it does mimic the horizontal force production in running. This exercise could be classified as SLT and functional

SLT matches perfectly the type of training performed on the SB. For example, if a person can perform 8 repetitions with 45 lb. dumbbells on bench presses, they will only get a fraction of that on a stability ball. Why? Due to the additional stabilization demands. Therefore, the individual was limited by the stabilization requirement not by the strength of the major chest musculature. Therefore, the name SLT applies quite nicely.

33. Dumbbell incline bench two arms alternating

It's virtually impossible to handle the same amount of weight on a SB incline DB press as on a regular bench, especially with an alternating pattern.

The purpose of SLT is the same as all functional training, to reduce the deficit in force production caused by the additional stabilization. As the deficit in force production is reduced (i.e. you are able to perform as many reps on the stability ball as you do on a bench), the joint integrity and stabilization increases. This allows one to produce more force in familiar tasks (e.g. a standard bench press) or more challenging environments (e.g. the playing field).

Stability Ball Training Safety Issues

Safety is of major concern when considering any training methodology. Therefore, it is mandatory that we dedicate a portion of this book to the safety issues concerning SB training.

Progression

One of the key components of training we always emphasize is ***proper progression*** of training. This basically refers to the "crawling before you walk" principle of teaching any skill. SB training is a skill. Thus, advancing a client through the proper progressions of an exercise not only ensures safety and effectiveness, but also promotes "learning through success." This approach promotes safety, program adherence, client retention and results.

A common concern amongst some fitness professionals is the fear that SB training is too advanced for some populations, like the geriatric population. The progressions we have developed for each body provides a wide range of intensity. The beginning version of each exercise is appropriate for the geriatric population. These exercises typically involve the short lever made possible by executing exercise from a kneeling position (e.g. push-ups), or with ball under the thighs or knees (e.g. Push-ups – hands on floor or supine bridges). As the progressions advance in difficulty, they can challenge the most accomplished athletes we have worked with. The advanced version of each exercise will usually involve a longer lever and minimum support base.

The primary focus should be on client safety. Always err on the conservative side when progressing a client. You can always speed the progression up. However, if an overzealous approach results in an injury, weeks and months of great training can be lost – not to mention the health of your client and their faith in your ability.

Ball size

Selecting a ball is simple. The SB size that is most versatile is one that will allow the user to sit on it with knees and hips at 90 degrees. However, using different size SBs will allow you more versatility and variation with your SB training. The different ball sizes allow body weight to be shifted in the appropriate direction to remove or add weight to any exercise.

Notice the 90 degree of hip and knee flexion when sitting on the ball.

The size of the SB can also be taken into account for flexibility differences amongst users. Many stretches can be supported by the SB in positions not otherwise possible.

In this chest and abdominal stretch, the more pronounced curvature of the smaller ball make the stretch more severe. The larger the ball, the less risk of hyper-extending the spine, especially with people who are limited in this flexibility (e.g. geriatrics).

Clothing

Always exercise with a shirt. Although several SB exercise videos show their models exercising without a shirt or in tank tops, exercising with these garments (or lack of) increase the chances for injury. Exercise will naturally cause sweating. A sweaty body can easily slide off the ball causing serious injury, especially if one falls while holding weight overhead. A shirt will also prevent the spreading of germs and bacteria to a minimum.

SB cleaning and pressure maintenance

If the SB is being used in the gym setting, keeping it clean with soap and water will also maintain proper sanitary conditions in the training environment and prevent the spread of germs and bacteria amongst clients and gym members. Keep the ball pumped with enough air to provide a firm surface. The more air pressure in the ball, the more support it will provide. The less air in the ball, the less stable it becomes.

External Support

I do not use any type of support or anchors to support limbs when training with the SB. The whole idea is to train in an unstable environment. The additional weight that can be handled when stabilizing the ball adds to the risk of an accident. I recommend training in an *unstable* training environment that is why I use the SB. If I need to train higher volumes with more aggressive intensities, I use the stable environment provided by a bench.

External resistance

When using external resistance, I recommend handling lighter loads than you would normally, when training on a standard bench. I do not recommend using high loads to failure on the SB – it's dangerous and does not promote to proper execution. While on a SB, an accident due to fatigue or technique error can happen too fast, even for a spotter to correct. The exercise should be terminated at first sign of technical error or fatigue.

Spotting

Spotters are recommended when using external resistance on the stability ball, especially when using loads that are challenging. However, if you are using appropriate loads and good form, minimal supervision is required. Even moderate loads will provide significant stabilization stimuli. Remember, that training should be fun and ultimately is a process for performance enhancement – it is not a contest to see who can handle the most weight!

Basic Teaching Cues and Recommendations

Teaching cues are a very personal thing. What works for one individual may do nothing for another. This section will provide some of the general cues we use everyday with our clients. We will also explore some of the concepts that have resulted in the development of many of the exercise cues used in the fitness industry (e.g. neutral spine). Regardless of the method of teaching you use to get your point across to a client, make sure the exercise environment is pain free, sensible, enjoyable and most of all, safe.

Neutral Spine

Unless otherwise specified, a neutral alignment of the spine should be maintained when exercising. This is especially critical when it comes to the lumbar spine and prone exercises. The key is to try and prevent the core musculature from disengaging and allowing a hyperextension of the lumbar spine during compression or flexion loading. A *"neutral spine"* is preferred when exercising, although occasionally we will ask for a posteriorly tilted pelvis during specific movements, i.e. a push-up or roll-out. This is done to teach preferential recruitment of specific musculature and provide a margin of safety for the lumbar spine. After proper core stabilization is mastered during the exercises, we no longer insist on a posterior pelvic tilt during the execution prone exercises. This process is not taught - it just evolves naturally. We teach a posterior pelvic tilt during prone exercises like the roll-outs and push-ups. The client eventually has the control to position the pelvis where it "feels" stable and comfortable (i.e. neutral).

Robinson defines a neutral spine as "a position or range of movement defined by the patient's symptoms, pathology, and current musculoskeletal restrictions. It is a position in which a vertical force exerted through the spine allows equal weight transference to the weight bearing surfaces (e.g. in sitting – the ischial tuberosities, in standing – the feet)." It should be noted that a neutral spine is an ideal concept defined differently by various authorities. A neutral spine is also different from person to person, therefore, don't get too caught up in the "exactness" of the definition and just use the concept! We always start with "pain free" execution and work from there.

When suspended in prone positions that load flexion of the spine (e.g. push-up or roll-out position), an attempt to maintain a slight posterior pelvic tilt engages the lower abdominals and prevents the lumbar spine from hyper-extending. This is the safety margin we want to develop up front. Although maintaining a "neutral spine" position during such exercises will provide adequate protection to the lumbar spine, the position is "too close for comfort" and can easily result in lumbar hyperextension in a fatigued state, especially for beginners. A posterior pelvic tilt provides better stimuli to the lower abdominals and hip flexors, and affords "more room for error." We also want to make sure our clients understand the importance of keeping a tight core with a natural drawing in of the abdominals. Our cure is "belly through the spine." If you look at most of our clients exercising in a prone position, you will see a natural line at their lumbar spine not a posterior pelvic tilt.

Notice that neither Diane nor I have a posterior pelvic tilt during these push-ups.
We are able to maintain a neutral pelvic line during the exercise.

Now let's take a close look at each body part and offer some general recommendations for positioning:

1) **Head** (ball under hips)

The cervical spine, or neck, should not be hyper flexed or extended. Try to maintain it in the position used when you are standing - in a neutral position. A general exception to this would be if the head needs to be moved to avoid hitting a surface, like a push-up with your feet on the ball (i.e. the neck may extend a bit more to realize a deeper push-up and avoid your face from hitting the ground).

2) **Core** (ball under hips, knees and feet progression)

When performing exercises where the body is suspended in the prone position between two distal support-points, it is imperative that the core be strong enough to maintain a posterior or neutral pelvic tilt. This protects the lumbar spine from hyperextension and requires exceptional abdominal and hip flexor strength. Strive for a straight body alignment from head to toe. See above picture).

3) **Abdominal strength and test**

A simple method of assessing abdominal strength is to check if a person can maintain their lower back flat to the ground when lifting one knee and foot off the ground.

Place the trainee on their back. Have them bend their knees and place their feet and shoulders flat on the ground. Have them press their lumbar spine against the ground. A ruler can be used to assure the lumbar spine is in contact with the ground at all times. Insert the ruler under the lumbar spine and have the individual pinch the ruler against the ground. Try to lift one keen off the ground while keep your lumbar spine falt to the ground. If you can pull the ruler out during the test, the lower abdominals have not been able to maintain a posterior pelvic tilt (i.e. has not maintained a flat lower back) – this means the lower abdominals and/or hip flexors are relatively weak. If an individual cannot maintain a flat lower back during this test, they should not perform advanced exercises that risk lumbar hyperextension, such as the rollouts (i.e. loaded flexion in a prone position). This test can then be advanced to two knees and eventually to extended leg (s).

4) **Protraction/Retraction**

Finally, exercises requiring the arms to support the weight of the body demand optimal integrity of the shoulder complex. The key element to look for is proper stabilization of the scapula and thoracic complexes. An individual should be able to prevents scapular "collapse". Holding a slightly, retracted (i.e. pre-stretched) position will allow more force production on a bench press, especially since the bench supports the scapulas and prevent their separation from the rib cage. During pronated exercises on the SB, the ability to produce maximum force is superceded by joint stabilization. Therefore, a stable scapular complex is needed for optimal performance. Retraction and protraction can be emphasized in an isolated manner to teach recruitment patterns which can then be incorporated in normal pressing mechanics.

This retracted position can be part of deliberate retraction and protraction exercises. However, this position should be avoided when stabilizing the shoulder complex during presses (e.g. Push-ups)

5) **Standing Exercises**

When exercising in a standing position, there are a few teaching cues which will help make the learning and training process flow smoothly. During wall slides, the middle of the stability ball should be at about the belt line. This ball position will provide adequate support at the bottom position of a squat.

Notice the beginning position of the ball. This "belt line" position allows proper stabilization and balance throughout the exercise.

When performing freestanding, single leg exercises, smaller balls require less flexibility on the part of the trailing leg's hip flexors. Since a deeper squat is possible, a smaller SB places a higher strength demand on the part of the ground-leg hip extensors. Larger balls require greater hip flexor flexibility but reduce the range of motion, placing less emphasis on the ground-based leg strength.

Obviously, the two-leg position of any exercise should be mastered before the one-leg version is attempted.

Single leg exercises require less flexibility when smaller balls are used. However, they allow a deeper squat that requires more strength.

Progressive Resistance and Flexibility on the Stability Ball

SB training provides several inherent advantages that are not available through other methods of strength training. Training on a SB provides versatility in the amount of resistance and flexibility that an exercise can provide without changing weight or equipment. Let's look at some SB training concepts that will allow you unparalleled diversity in your progressions.

Prone lever system

One of the advantages of SB training is that it uses the body's lever system to allow variation in resistance. This inherent lever system can take into account the core stability of an individual while adjusting the resistance applied to the prime movers at the extremities. More importantly, SB training allows the lever system to change while performing an exercise. This is something that is virtually impossible to do while on a resistance training machine.

The lever system can be used to make exercises easier as one fatigues. Above, a straight arm rollout can be stepped down in intensity by going to a forearm/elbow support.

Away from the arms, the demand for core stability is increased as well as the weight the arms and chest must support. The longer the distance between the support points (in this instant the ball and arms) the harder the exercises will be. The natural progression for the "hands on floor" push-up is:

1. SB under the hips
2. SB under the thighs
3. SB under the knees
4. SB under the shins, and
5. SB under the feet.

Notice the lever arm of this exercise getting larger as the SB gets closer to the feet. This increases the strength demands of the upper body, as well as the core of the body.

Repeating this sequence, using a single-leg support can advance this progression to challenge the most advanced clients. This application will be discussed further in the section addressing bases of support progression

Leg position for stabilization progression

The width of the support at the legs can also provide adjustments in the demand of an exercise. A wide leg position offers greater support and the wider support makes an exercise easier. As the legs get closer to each other, there is less of a support base making the exercise harder. This concept applies to all SB exercises regardless of ball position. Ultimately, 1 leg-supported exercises are the hardest due to the additional support and balance demands. Careful attention should be paid to stabilizing the hips in a stable and leveled position, preventing lumbar hyperextension and core or hip rotation. Master an exercise using a wide foot position then narrow the base of support until one leg support can be executed. Abducting the free leg during the single leg version of any exercise really challenges transverse plane stabilization on sagittal plane dominant exercises (e.g. push-up).

Reducing contact area of support

Reducing the contact surface of any supporting limb can increase the load and neural demand of any exercise, especially where the hands or legs contact the ball. As mentioned earlier, two-leg support is easier than one-leg support. You can then proceed from thigh, shin or instep support to the balls of the feet. Finally, the contact area on the stability ball can be further reduced by going to toe stabilization position (i.e. 2 feet to single foot).

Single leg support can add an enormous amount of intensity to any prone exercise – especially if the toes provide the support. This progression puts double the pressure on the hip flexors of the support side and challenges the internal and external rotators of the hip.

The same approach can be taken when we support the upper body on the SB using the arms. Elbow/forearm stabilization (e.g. as in roll-outs) is easier than hand support. Two factors play a role here; lever arm and support based surface area. Two-hand stabilization (e.g. as in lockout stabilization and push-ups) can be made more challenging by going to a single hand progression. While a two hand version of many exercises can be executed safely by many individuals, the single arm versions are extreme applications requiring advance training.

Increased flexibility and strength demand

Using various size stability balls allows one to vary the flexibility demands of many exercises. For example, during the single-leg squat progression, the free leg is being supported by the ball. Smaller balls require less flexibility from the adductors or hip flexors of the SB support leg. While smaller balls require less flexibility, they allow a deeper squat which increases the need for leg and hip strength of the ground-based leg. For flexibility work, choose the smallest ball available to start then, progress to larger balls requiring the greatest amount of hip flexor flexibility. For strength work, start on a large ball then work to smaller balls that allow the deeper squat.

The lever system is not only affected by the sized of the ball, but also by ball placement. The closer the ball is to the mainline of the body during single leg exercises, the less flexibility and stabilization is needed. The further the ball is from the ground-support foot, the greater the requirement for stabilization and flexibility.

The larger the ball on the single leg SB squat the more flexibility is needed from the hip flexors of the SB support side.

During the single-leg squat progression, start with "stationary" free leg support. This requires less balance. Then, advance to dynamic movement, varying the distance between the support foot and the ball.

Once you have advanced to the dynamic single-leg squat progression, a "foot to mid-lower-leg role" adds a bit of stability in terms of ball position. The action and speed of the exercise will dominate the stability requirements. If you do not have perfect execution during this dynamic exercise, the ball will role the "free leg" off. This "roll" again adds to the transverse plane stabilization requirements

Ball size also affects flexibility in other exercises such as pike shoulder presses and some of the stretches. Stretches like the supine abdominal stretch are supported to a greater extent by the larger size balls. In the pike shoulder press, larger balls require less hamstring and glute flexibility. However, these tucked positions provide greater vertical positions (e.g. more weight supported by the upper body) requiring more upper body strength for proper execution. This is one of the many reasons I recommend that everyone use several different size stability balls. It adds more versatility and range to your training.

Notice the greater amount of hamstring flexibility required by the smaller ball (top). The larger ball requires less flexibility, but puts a greater amount of load on the upper body (below).

Complimentary equipment

As versatile as the SB is, its versatility is further enhanced when it is incorporated with other training equipment. We have successfully incorporated the SB with rubber tubing, various medicine balls, dumbbells, side-angled boxes (i.e. "sidestrike"), and other balance equipment, such as rocker boards.

Resistance training in an unstable environment

Performing resistance training on the SB is a great way to work on stabilization and neural efficiency. The SB can be used in the same fashion as a bench. This application allows a series of squatting, lunging, pressing, and pulling exercises. The unstable environment created by the stability ball requires superior balance and stabilization on the part of the core and stabilizing structures. Changing the contraction pattern will change the center of mass and increase the balance requirements of any exercise. As stated previously, due to the increased balance requirement of this type of training, I do not recommend extremely heavy loads to failure, or barbell work. Before embarking on this type of approach to stability ball training, the trainee should first be taught how to "miss a lift" and drop the weights to the side. This awareness creates a more confident training environment. I do recommend spotting with beginners until they have mastered the essence of this method of training. However, if the training has been progressed properly, little supervision is needed if starting loads are light and emphasis is on form rather than weight lifted.

Rubber Tubing

Rubber tubing can be used to create horizontal resistance for exercise such as rowing or resisted rotations. The SB can be used as a seat, or a supine support, during these types of exercises. This "unstable" exercise environment adds to the neurological demand of the activity. Our geriatric clients are usually challenged by sitting on the ball using a two-leg ground base support, while a single leg ground support further challenges more advanced trainees. With the assistance of a partner or trainer, the line of pull can be changed without notice to further challenge the stabilization and reflex postural adjustments of the core.

MB Training

Medicine balls can also be incorporated into your SB training. Medicine balls come in weights ranging from 2 to 40 pounds. They also have various gripping capabilities, such as handles and ropes. They also come in different textures and bounce qualities. This makes them suitable for any population and creates a very safe form of resistance training.

Medicine balls can be used just like any other type of resistance and the SB can be incorporated just as you would a bench. Just about any exercise you can imagine with a barbell can be performed with a medicine ball. However, due to their rubber make-up, they can also be thrown (e.g. incorporating an overhead throw with an abdominal crunch, while sitting on the ball). This versatility allows one to address the dynamic nature of postural adjustments typical in speed and power dominated events, such as reactions to falls in the senior population and sport specific movements in athletes. The handles on "Power-Balls" allow these medicine balls to be used like dumbbells. The rope attachments on the "Converta-Balls" add a whole dimension to this training, allowing you to perform a variety of swinging exercises while sitting on the SB.

Balance equipment

The SB can be seen as a piece of balance equipment in itself. However, there are other pieces of balance equipment that can be incorporated with the SB to add diversity and fun to your training. For example, Biofoam rollers and rocker boards can be used at the opposite extremities of the SB to increase balance requirements during push-ups and sitting balance exercises. This application makes for a great "game-oriented environment" for youth as well as experienced trainees.

Stability Ball Training:
Application and Integration

Anytime a new revolutionary methodology is developed there is always resistance from traditionalists. This is true in most industries and the fitness industry is no different. Therefore, the **3 Tier Integration System (3TIS)** was developed as a method of introducing "non-traditional" functional training into existing and more "conventional" training models. Why did we develop the 3TIS? We realize the importance of integration of various training methods, "no one training methodology does everything." An integrated model of training will always provide the most effective training stimuli.

One of the populations SB training has had some opposition from is the power athlete/coach. The primary argument is that large loads cannot be handled using SBs. Large loads, accompanied with large training volumes are needed to create the hormonal and mechanical stress conducive to the development of hypertrophy and absolute strength gains. These two qualities are the barometer by which many athletes are gauged by, and many contracts hinge on. Therefore, the reluctance to embrace SB training by conditioning professionals who work with this population of athletes is understandable. A model was needed to allow functional training modalities (e.g. stability ball training), to be integrated into traditional strength and hypertrophy training models.

One of the reasons stability ball training has become so popular is that it compliments traditional training methodology so well. Many of the injuries we see within aggressive training models are due primarily to, 1) over-training and 2) lack of joint stabilization. Both of these issues are automatically addressed when using the SLT methodology inherent to the SB. The 3TIS offers a way to complimentarily use functional training, with the standard hypertrophy and strength training. You can indeed get the best of both training approaches!

The 3TIS provides three levels of integration; as a **warm-up or cool down**, as a **build-up** to work intensity and as a method of **unloading**. This integration model allows the main objectives of conventional training approaches to be realized (e.g. hypertrophy and absolute strength development), while deriving the benefits of SB and functional training. This is certainly an example of how "the whole is greater than the sum of its parts". Now, lets go over the three levels of integration in more detail.

Warm-up/Cool down

The easiest way to introduce SB training to anyone is in the warm up. Most trainees are more willing to experiment with new training approaches and new exercises a few minutes before their "workout." This is a great way to introduce this method of training into a traditional program without taking away the program emphasis. Using this level of integration, the conditioning professional can implement a stretching routine, or exercises geared to warm the body in a couple of ways. The intensity and difficulty of this warm-up session can be tailored to the specific population being worked with. We have often engaged our clients during this warm session in a manner where they have voluntarily elected to increase the stabilization and balance component of their workouts.

Stretching protocols on the SB offer several advantages over traditional stretching routines. Due to the unstable nature of the stability ball, stretching on it carries a high balance component. The ability to simultaneously train balance and flexibility makes this application very time efficient. The SB also allows extreme positions to be supported during the flexibility application. Without the gentle support of the SB, many stretches (e.g. supine abdominal/chest stretch, adductor stretch and the lunge hip flexor stretch) would not be possible for individuals lacking the supportive strength necessary to hold these positions. This type of flexibility training eventually develops the strength needed to hold these positions without the aid of the SB – strength and flexibility you can use. The dynamic nature of SB stretching can range from slow to ballistic. It offers and intensity range for any application!

The SB provides support and residual balance training, making it a safe and efficient way to warm-up or cool-down.

Another way to use the SB in the warm-up is by developing total body warm-up protocols. We call these ***compound warm-ups***. By designing a sequence of specific movements, the needs of any individual (e.g. neural re-education, weakness, imbalance, or lack of flexibility) or the demands of the upcoming training session can be addressed.

The moves are choreographed in such a way where the trainee flows from one exercise to the other with very little or no rest. The length of the compound and difficulty of the exercises can be tailored to match the training capacity of any individual. Here is a sample of a compound warm-up from our upcoming programming chapter.

Compound #2 Intermediate (Prone –Ball on Ground)
1. Walk-outs
2. Push-ups (hands on floor)
3. Log rolls
4. Knee tucks
5. Hypers

1   2   3   4   5

Finally, SB training can also be used as a warm up to a specific body part. This is accomplished by performing an equivalent, or similar exercise on the SB to warm up the specific body part to be worked. Using the bench press as an example, the trainee can perform a few sets using DBs on the stability ball then go straight to the target intensity on the bench press. The warm-up intensity on the SB should be kept light enough to perform multiple sets at the rep range described by the periodization phase of the current training the cycle (e.g. 8-12 for hypertrophy, 3-6 for strength, etc.). Here is an example of a specific warm-up.

Specific #4 Chest (Body weight)
1. Walk outs
2. Push-ups (hands on ground)
3. Walk back
4. Push-ups (hands on ball)
5. Lateral Rocking push-ups – this exercise was developed after the ESBT volumes were produced. Roll the ball from side to side while you are doing a push-up so that one side of body is emphasized. This progression teaches the balance necessary for a single arm push-up.

| 1 | 2 | 3 | 4 | 5 |

Although this may seem like a small amount of work, neurophysiology research by Wolpaw, Aosaki and others, as well as our observations, begin to shed some light on the process of neural and reflex engramming (i.e. skill acquisition). Some of their work shows that structural changes in the higher orders of the CNS can start within minutes of the introduction of a novel skill. Therefore, we feel that a 10-15 minute session can yield remarkable results in as little as a couple of weeks. This is consistent with our observations.

Build-up

The second level of integration is the build-up. Using the build-up method is by far the best way to "transfer" the absolute strength developed with more traditional exercises to a more functional application. Thus, the build-up is a very effective method of reducing the deficit between absolute and functional strength.

This approach is very similar to the "body part warm-up" method previously discussed. However, the main difference between the two methods is one of intensity. In the build-up method, a traditional resistance-training exercise (e.g. DB Bench Press) is started on the stability ball. The load of each set should increase (i.e. the build-up) until you cannot perform the desired number of reps with good form. At this point, a few more "supported sets" can be performed on a stable environment (e.g. bench or machine) to work on absolute strength and hypertrophy. This method of integration very closely resembles the "pre-exhaustion" method of training developed in the late 60s and early 70s.

The main purpose of this strategy is to reduce the difference between the weight used in the unstable environment and the stable environment (i.e. deficit). In essence, develops more usable strength. Here is an example of a build-up – more protocols are forthcoming in the next chapter.

Build-up #1 Legs
1.DB One leg SB Squat with mobility
2.DB Lunges or step-ups

One leg SB squats (above) are perfect for "building up" to heavy reaching (below) or traditional lunges.

Unloading

The final level of integration within the 3TIS model is the unloading application. The main concept behind this method of implementation is to allow the prime movers to be targeted for heavy traditional strength/hypertrophy training on one day of the week, and unload with functional training on lighter days. This unloading principle is typical of most training models where "sub-threshold intensities" are used on alternating sessions to allow fatigued muscle to recover. Here is an example of the unloading method of integration.

Unloading #5 Shoulders
1.Heavy BB Overhead Presses on Tuesday
2.SB Pike presses on Friday

Heavy, overhead presses (above) can be unloaded by Pike SB presses (below). The SB exercise will be limited by core strength so the shoulders will get a break from the heavy work.

Using SB training to unload muscle groups previously fatigued during past training sessions provides several advantages. First, it provides the active recovery which research has indicated facilitates faster restoration after training. Second, it provides stabilization work needed to support high-volume and high intensity training. Third, it provides additional training volume associated with muscle hypertrophy and physiological conditioning. Finally, although the unloading day may not provide the prime movers with traditional heavy work, the neurological demand of stability ball exercises still maintain a high level of intensity.

The 3TIS of training offers a solution to the never-ending conflict between tradition and innovation. More importantly, it provides a model of integration between training modalities that are not mutually exclusive, rather it is inter-related and complimentary to each other.

Stability Ball Training Programming

As with any other exercise program design, it is not an exact science. In many ways, program design is an art. A good understanding of physiology, exercise training, variable manipulation, common sense, and creativity are the starting ingredients necessary to successfully apply this training methodology. The best way to start is just to dive into it with some common sense. Try all exercises before coaching them. This way you will have a preview of the concerns your clients and athletes will have. You will know in advance the sticking points of the exercises and develop possible coaching cues to help individuals through them.

Preparation considerations

As with any type of training, a proper warm-up is essential to prepare the body for work. The whole idea of the warm up is to increase core temperature so that muscles will become more pliable and elastic. This prepares the body for movement and reduces the risk of soft tissue injuries. The warm-up should proceed from general to specific movements.

Although The Essence of Stability Ball Training (ESBT) videos shows a combination of biomotor skills being used as a warm-up modality, stationary bikes, treadmills and other pieces of aerobic equipment are also suitable.

Below is a list of biomotor skills we used as an active warm up in the ESBT. These drills are appropriate for healthy, asymptomatic individuals and illustrate some examples of what can be done in a small area.
1) **Running in place**
2) **Butt kickers**
3) **Jumping jacks (various)**
4) **Stationary skips (various)**
5) **Wood Chop**
6) **Twists**
7) **Diagonal wood chops**
8) **Circles**

Taking about 15-20 seconds to perform each exercise will provide about 2 minutes of an aerobic warm-up. This should be sufficient to start elevating core temperature to prepare the body for a more specific warm up incorporating the SB.

Individuals with orthopedic limitations can skip the ground-based higher impact skills and try some light bouncing on the SB while in a sitting position. If orthopedically tolerated, this gentle bouncing provides good balance and core training, while stimulating the cardiovascular system. This is a great warm-up option for the geriatric population.

Flexibility Exercises and Application

The following SB flexibility exercises will prepare the body for further work. Flexibility work on the SB requires more balance than floor stretching, adding residual balance training to the warm-up. You should perform various repetitions of each of these stretching exercises for about 15-20 seconds. This will provide your warm-up with an additional 4 to 5 minutes of specific work

1) **Anterior and Posterior Hip tilts**
2) **Lateral Hip tilts**
3) **Hip circles (clock/counter)**
4) **Lateral adductor**
5) **Side oblique → Mobility oblique**
6) **Curl-up → Toe touch → Alternating leg**
7) **Split lunge hip flexor → Glute and Periformis**
8) **Supine abdominal/chest stretch**
9) **Rotations → Mobility**
10) **Supine Side to Side lateral rolls**
11) **Prone spinal rolls**
12) **Hip flexor stretch**
13) **Posterior Shoulder**
14) **Prone core rocking**
15) **Shoulder roll out → Rotations**

Individuals with limiting orthopedic considerations or other health concerns, may select 3-4 exercises from the stretching list and perform each for 2-3 minutes. This will still provide 6-12 minutes of preparation for heavier exercise.

Flexibility protocols
Flexibility protocols can be put together to emphasize a specific need or for general flexibility. As previously mentioned, flexibility work with the SB is much more then stretching. SB flexibility protocols provide balance, coordination, functional range of motion and strength. Since it greatly involves the CNS in terms of skill acquisition, the improvements are dramatic and rapid.

#1 Novice/Geriatric
➢ Hip circles (clock/counter)   NOTES:
➢ Curl-up → Toe touch → Alternating leg
➢ Supine abdominal/chest stretch
➢ Prone spinal rolls
➢ Posterior Shoulder

#2 Intermediate
➢ Hip circles (clock/counter)   NOTES:
➢ Side oblique → Mobility oblique
➢ Split lunge hip flexor → Glute and Periformis
➢ Prone core rocking

Warm-up Application and Protocols
The following are some examples of warm up protocols we have used with our clients. We have separated them into two groups, compound warm-ups and specific

warm-ups. Compound warm-ups will string a sequence of exercises that will cover the entire body.

The first rule and only rule of designing compounds is "there are no rules – just reasons." That means, "as long as you have a logical and sound purpose for your specific design, you are good to go." After all, it's your design! However, the key is to be SOUND and LOGICAL.

Let's look at a few compounds and see how they differ in intensity. Next to the number I have indicated what population the compound is suitable for. I have also tried to provide some cues as to hand and ball positioning. This should make it easier to envision the body position and exercise movement. Remember these are just examples and by no means are prescriptions for your specific clients. Make sure that you are aware of specific contra-indications, adhere to sound training principles and error on the side of conservatism.

Compound #1 Novice/Geriatric
Ball on wall
➢ Front wall slide (~70 degree incline)   NOTES:
➢ Push-ups (hands on ball – at chest height)
➢ Roll-up (hands on ball at head height)
➢ Hypers (Ball at navel)

Compound #2 Intermediate
Prone –Ball on Ground
➢ Walk-outs   NOTES:
➢ Push-ups (hands on floor)
➢ Log rolls
➢ Knee tucks
➢ Hypers

Compound #3 Advanced/Athlete
Ball on wall
➢ One leg squat (Stationary ball support)   NOTES:
➢ Push-ups (hands on ball)
➢ Roll-outs (knees or foot support)
➢ Twisters
➢ Hypers (Ball at navel)

Compound #4 DBs – pressing emphasis
Standing →Sitting →Lying on ball
➢ One leg squat (Stationary ball support)   NOTES:
➢ Sitting DB Bent-over laterals
➢ Sitting DB Up-right (alternating)
➢ DB Chest Fly (Alternating)
➢ DB Supine rotations
➢ Diagonal Pullovers

Specific #1 Legs
Wall slide
- Two leg back wall slide – to one leg
- Side wall slide to - to one leg
- Front wall slide – to one leg

NOTES:

Specific #2 Legs
Standing
- One leg – to mobility
- Lateral one leg - to mobility
- Lateral one leg- to rotational reach
- Hypers (Ball at navel)

NOTES:

Specific #3 Legs/hips
Supine and Prone
- Prone two leg extension – to one leg
- Pikes – hands on ground
- Supine leg curl – to one leg
- Supine bridges – to one leg

NOTES:

Specific #4 Chest
Body weight
- Walk outs
- Push-ups (hands on ground)
- Walk back
- Push-ups (hands on ball)
- Lateral Rocking push-ups

NOTES:

Specific #5 Chest/Shoulders
External resistance
- DB Shoulder Press (sitting on ball)
- DB Alternating Incline Press
- DB Alternating Flyes

NOTES:

Specific #5 Back
Bodyweight
- Hypers with compound Ys
- Elbow rollouts from knees (hands together)
- Posterior shoulder stretch

NOTES:

Specific #6 Back
External resistance
- Dumbbell Rowing (2 DB simultaneously)   NOTES:
- 1 DB Rowing with mobility
- Alternating DB Pull-overs

Build–up Application and Protocols s

As stated before, build-ups help to transfer the strength developed in more traditional exercises to a more functional method of expression. They are an effective method of reducing the deficit between absolute and functional strength. Many traditional resistance-training exercises can be started on the SB. Build-ups can start as a warm-up. However, they go beyond just warm-up. The intensities reached during SB build-ups surpass those used in a warm-up method of integration. The loads go as high as good form will allow. At this point, the first work set of the "stabilized" exercise can be performed. Let's take a look at some of the build-ups we have successfully used over the past few years.

Build-up #1 Legs
- One leg SB Squat with DBs   NOTES:
- DB Lunges or step-ups

Build-up #2 Legs
- Weighted SB wall slide (may need partner)   NOTES:
- Squats

Build-up #3 Chest
- DB SB Presses (flat or incline)   NOTES:
- BB Bench press (flat or incline)

Build-up #4 Shoulders
- Sitting SB DB Uprights   NOTES:
- Standing Alternating DB Uprights

Build-up #5 Shoulders
- SB 1Arm bend-over row (free hand on ball)   NOTES:
- 1 Arm DB Rows "free hand on bench"

Unloading Application and Protocols

The "unloading system" allows the prime movers to be targeted for heavy traditional strength/hypertrophy one day of the week and unloaded with functional training on lighter days. The following are some of the unloading schemes that can be implemented with the stability ball.

42

Unloading #1 Legs
➤ Heavy Squats on Tuesday
➤ 1 Leg SB Wall Slide on Friday

NOTES:

Unloading #2 Legs
➤ Lateral lunges on Monday
➤ Lateral One-leg SB Squat on Thursday

NOTES:

Unloading #3 Chest
➤ Heavy Bench on Tuesday
➤ Alternating SB DB Flyes on Friday

NOTES:

Unloading #4 Chest
➤ Heavy Incline DB Presses on Monday
➤ Large SB Roller Coasters on Thursday

NOTES:

Unloading #5 Shoulders
➤ Heavy Presses BN on Tuesday
➤ SB Tucked Shoulder presses on Friday

NOTES:

Unloading #5 Shoulders
➤ Heavy Uprights or Cleans on Monday
➤ SB Seated Upright DB Rows on Thursday

NOTES:

Unloading #6 Back
➤ Pull-ups on Monday
➤ SB Elbow Roll-outs on Thursday

NOTES:

Unloading #7 Back
➤ Cable Rows on Tuesday
➤ SB DB Rows (chest on ball) Friday

NOTES:

Transitional Application and Protocols

The transitional application of the SB is another great way to introduce this training modality. Many times, two to three minutes of rest are taken between heavy resistance training exercises. During this time, many people walk around, drink water, or talk with friends.   Not our clients!   We use active "transitions" as rest periods. Transitions can be balance work, light antagonist work, flexibility work, postural core training or training another body part. It resembles circuit work, but provides the body with active recovery during the transition.

Many people are concerned about fatiguing the CNS. This is a legitimate concern, but not with the SB. At first, you definitely want to go easy with the SB transitions – you seen how much energy goes into learning how to ride a bike… At first, it is absolutely exhausting. The entire body is tense as muscles are fighting against one another instead of cooperating with each other. However, soon after the initial learning stage, riding a bike becomes effortless and even relaxing. Plus, once you've done it, it's yours forever. It's the same with the SB. At first, learning to balance and control one's body on the SB is an arduous task. However, once you learn the skill, it's easy to do and yours for life – just like riding a bike! So, start easy and then just add on to the transitional method of integration. Your traditional workouts will take on a new look and feel. The following are some of the transitions we use with our clients.

Transition #1

- Heavy Squats
- Sitting/kneeling balance on SB
- Prone rolls

NOTES:

Transition #2

- Bench press
- Compound Ys
- Posterior shoulder stretch on SB

NOTES:

Transition #3

- Pull-ups
- SB Push-ups (hands on ball)
- Shoulder rotation rolls

NOTES:

Sample Workouts

The aim of this chapter is to illustrate how SB exercises can be combined to create total body workouts. The following pages provide a look at three training routines utilizing the SB. These routines are examples of how the concepts discussed earlier can be applied in developing safe and progressive programs. These workouts consist of 8 different movement components. Each movement component is associated with a major system of muscles. At the end we have a balance component that always adds a smile to the client's face. The programs can be performed in succession (i.e. complete all sets of one exercise before going to the next exercise), or as a sequenced circuit (i.e. all 8 exercises performed one after another). Performing 3 sets of each exercise for 5-15 reps can serve as a general guideline to volume. The number of reps will depend on the proficiency and technique of the trainee, as well as the intensity of the exercises.

Warm-up before your workout. Use any one of the protocols provided in the Warm-up Protocol section to prepare for the main portion of the training session. Individuals with orthopedic limitations can skip higher impact skills and try some light flexibility work on the SB. If orthopedically tolerated, gentle bouncing provides good balance and core training, while increasing core temperature and respiratory rates. It is one of our favorite ways to warm up our geriatric clients. Make sure you select an exercise with the client's limitations in mind. Advance only through successful execution of an exercise and you will eliminate unnecessary risks.

To add a bit more variety to your programming, you can introduce balancing equipment, such as rocker boards and Air X pads. Balancing exercises can make a great transition and recovery station between exercises. With balancing, the trainer can teach recovery techniques, such as controlled breathing and relaxation. Mastering these components of can reduce the time one needs for recovery by increasing and enhancing the ability to restore systematic homeostasis.

Beginner

The following program is designed to introduce a beginner trainee to SB training and should be tolerated by most asymptomatic individuals. However, care should always be taken when tailoring a training program. Every individual is different with varying needs.

LEGS - SQUATTING

Exercise name: Back wall Slide.
Purpose: Teach proper squatting form and strengthen legs and hips.
Procedure: Put back against the wall. Place center of ball at your belt line. Squat down and stand back up.
Comments: Look straight ahead. Keep feet flat. Eventually, move feet back until you don't need the ball anymore to support you.

CHEST - PUSH

Exercise name: Push-up – legs on ball.
Purpose: Strengthen upper body push. Develop core and shoulder stability.
Procedure: Walk out until ball is below hips and perform push-ups.
Comments: Keep the entire body straight to prevent lumbar hyperextension. Move ball towards feet to increase intensity.

BACK -PULL

Exercise name: Seated rowing.

Purpose: Teach balance and strengthen pulling action.

Procedure: Sit on ball and grip handle of cable or band. Row using preferred method.

Comments: Face forward. Keep lumbar spine straight, feet flat and shoulder blades stable.

SHOULDER -PULL

Exercise name: DB Sitting upright row.

Purpose: Strengthen core and shoulders. Strengthen pulling from the floor while sitting action.

Procedure: Sit with an open stance. Row in an alternating fashion inside of the legs.

Comments: Keep belly button through the spine – core tight.

CORE - FLEXION

Exercise name: Floor crunches – feet on ball.

Purpose: Strengthen core. Teach the crunch movement and preferential recruitment of core musculature.

Procedure: Lay on floor, put legs on the ball as to keep hips and knees at 90 degrees of flexion. Crunch and bring shoulder blades off ground.

Comments: Keep eyes looking at ceiling to prevent flexion of the neck. The further the hand/arms are from the ball the higher the intensity.

CORE - EXTENSION

Exercise name: Two leg bridge.

Purpose: Strengthen core and hips. Teach balance.

Procedure: Lay down on floor with heels on the ball. Bridge the hips up to comfortable height.

Comments: Keep arms flat on floor and progress to arms across chest. Keep knees slightly bent at all times.

CORE - ROTATION

Exercise name: Floor supine rotation.

Purpose: Increase core rotational flexibility and strength.

Procedure: Lay on floor, put legs on the ball as to keep hips and knees at 90 degrees of flexion. Roll the ball sideways without lifting shoulder off the ground.

Comments: Keep shoulders on ground and movement controlled.

BALANCE

Exercise name: Sitting knee lifts.

Purpose: Teach ball balance and core stabilization.

Procedure: Sit on ball. Slowly lift knee and hold for 5-10 seconds.

      Comments: Keep facing forwards and belly button through the spine.

Intermediate

The intermediate program is appropriate for individuals who have mastered the basic balancing and functional strength components need for successful SB training. The intensity of the basic exercises have been increased by reducing the support base and increasing the lever arm of the basic exercises.

LEGS -SQUATTING
Exercise name: Back wall slide –one leg.
Purpose: Strengthen single leg stability and strength.
Procedure: Put back against the wall. Place center of ball at your belt line. Balance on one leg and squat down -stand back up.
Comments: Look straight ahead. Keep foot flat. Eventually, move foot back until you don't need the ball anymore to support you.

CHEST - PUSH
Exercise name: Push-up – hands on ball.
Purpose: Strengthen upper body push. Develop core and shoulder stability.
Procedure: Put hands on ball and walk your feet back to a push-up position.
Comments: Keep the entire body straight to prevent lumbar hyperextension.

BACK -PULL

Exercise name: DB Row – one arm on ball – feet staggered.

Purpose: Teach balance and standing, pulling action from floor.

Procedure: Place one arm on ball and walk feet back to a staggered position. Perform a single arm row.

Comments: Neutral cervical spine. Keep lumbar spine straight, feet flat and shoulder blades stable.

SHOULDER -PUSH

Exercise name: DB Sitting overhead press –one arm.

Purpose: Strengthen core and shoulders. Strengthen overhead pressing action.

Procedure: Sit with an open stance. Pick up DB and press overhead.

Comments: Keep belly button through the spine – core tight. Eyes forward.

CORE – FLEXION

Exercise name: Full abdominal crunch.

Purpose: Strengthen core. Teach the crunch movement and balance.

Procedure: Sit on ball, put feet on floor. Crunch to an upright position.

Comments: Keep cervical spine in neutral and prevent flexion of the neck. The further the hand/arms are from the hips the higher the intensity.

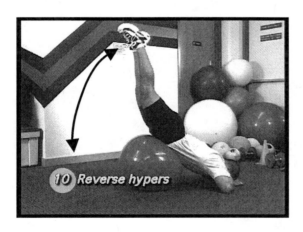

CORE - EXTENSION

Exercise name: Reverse hyperextension.

Purpose: Strengthen core and hips.

Procedure: Mount the ball so your hips are on top of the ball and your toes and elbows are touching the ground. Slowly lift heels off the ground as high as possible.

Comments: Keep heels and knees together. Move slowly through motion. Maintain upper body stable on the ground.

CORE - ROTATION
Exercise name: Supine resisted rotation.
Purpose: Increase core rotational flexibility, strength and balance.
Procedure: Lay on ball. Put ball between shoulder blades. Use wide stance and keep feet flat. Use band cable or medicine ball for resistance. Rotated through a 180 degree range, while balancing on the ball.
Comments: Keep hips up, feet flat and cervical spine neutral.

BALANCE
Exercise name: Four point balance.
Purpose: Teach ball balance.
Procedure: Put hands on floor and tuck so that the ball is under shins. Slowly bring one hand to the ball and off ground.
Comments: Alternate hand position until you can balance with both hands off ground.

Advanced

This advanced SB program requires superior balance and core strength to execute safely and effectively. Most athletes are challenged by it and only a few of our personal training clients are capable of completing all of the exercises. This program should be reserved only for the advanced training population.

LEGS -SQUATTING
Exercise name: One leg stability ball squat.
Purpose: Strengthen single leg stability and strength. Teach single leg reaches and squatting.
Procedure: Stand on one leg with the rear leg on the stability ball. Place ball under the shin of the rear leg. Squat down on the front leg while maintaining balance.
Comments: Look straight ahead. Keep front foot flat.

CHEST - PUSH
Exercise name: DB Flat bench press – two arm simultaneous.
Purpose: Strengthen upper body push. Develop core and shoulder stability.
Procedure: Sit on ball while holding DBs on knees. Roll back on ball while bringing DBs to chest. Press.
Comments: Keep cervical spine neutral and hips up. Core tight.

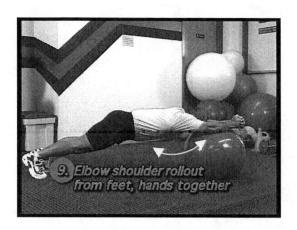

BACK -PULL

Exercise name: Rollout – on elbows.

Purpose: Teach pulling in a laid out position. Strengthen core.

Procedure: Balance on the ball with your elbows –in a push-up position. Roll elbows out as far as you can without losing core stability.

Comments: Keep entire body straight. Prevent lumbar hyperextension.

SHOULDER -PUSH

Exercise name: Pike press.

Purpose: Strengthen core and shoulders. Teach handstand.

Procedure: Get into a push-up position with ball under shins. Press into a pike position. Maintain pike and press as doing a handstand.

Comments: Keep belly button through the spine and a tight pike. Use a larger ball if hip and hamstring flexibility are an issue.

CORE - FLEXION

Exercise name: Resisted SB Crunch.

Purpose: Strengthen core. Teach the crunch movement and balance.

Procedure: Sit on ball, put feet on floor. Crunch to an upright position. Use any weighted object for resistance.

Comments: Keep cervical spine in neutral and prevent flexion of the neck. The further the hand/arms are from the hips the higher the intensity.

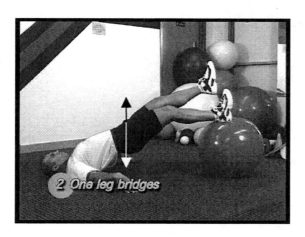

CORE - EXTENSION

Exercise name: One leg ball bridges.

Purpose: Strengthen core and hips. Strengthen running muscles.

Procedure: Lay on ground with the heel of one leg on top of the ball – keep free leg in air. Bridge hips as high as possible.

Comments: Keep support leg knee slightly bent. Move slowly through motion. Maintain upper body stable on the ground.

CORE - ROTATION

Exercise name: Prone skiers –two leg.

Purpose: Increase core rotational flexibility, strength and balance. Strengthen upper body during rotational activities.

Procedure: Assume a tucked position on ball – knees on top of ball with hands on ground. .

Comments: Keep hips up, feet flat and cervical spine neutral.

BALANCE

Exercise name: Two point kneeling balance.

Purpose: Teach ball balance and core stabilization.

Procedure: From a four point position (hands and shins on ball), slowly lift upper body as to balance on ball in a kneeling position.

Comments: Try to straighten body completely, from head to knees.

Circuit Application and Protocols

The stability ball lends itself perfectly to circuit training. There is no changing of equipment, no changing of weight and no adjustments. The protocol designs are endless. Your clients will never get bored with this method, and as for intensity, there is no superior form of training. The design we use is similar to the format used by such leaders in the fields and Vern Gambetta. Here is how we combine the "Burn with Vern" and the "Stabilize with Santana" protocols (just kidding☺). Here are two possibilities for circuit design.

1) Select three exercises. One for the lower body (e.g. Supine leg curls), core (e.g. SB crunch), and the upper body (e.g. SB Push-up). Perform ***all three*** exercises for 30 seconds with 15 seconds rest (transition) between each, followed by 60 seconds of a biomotor skill = 1 set. Rest between 1-2 minutes between each set. Perform 3 sets of each circuit x 3-5 different circuits.

Novice

SB – Upper Body exercise	15sec rest	SB Core exercise	15 sec rest	SB Lower Body exercise	60 sec Biomotor skill (e.g. box shuffle)	ONE SET

———▶

2) Select three exercises. One for the lower body (e.g. Wall slide), core (e.g. SB Hypers), and the upper body (e.g. Elbow rollout). Perform ***each*** exercise for 30 seconds with 15 seconds rest (transition) between each, followed by 60 seconds of a biomotor (e.g. skip rope) skill x 3 exercises = 1 set. Rest 3-5 minutes between each set. Perform 3 sets of each circuit x 3-5 different circuits.

Intermediate to advance - Cardio emphasis

SB - Upper Body exercise	60 sec Biomotor Skill (e.g.skip rope)	SB- Core exercise	60 sec Biomotor Skill (e.g.skip rope)	SB- Lower Body exercise	60 sec Biomotor Skill (e.g.skip rope)	ONE SET

Another application of stability ball circuit training follows a more conventional approach. This method requires several balls, preferably different sizes and inflation pressures. Each ball becomes a station with a different exercise. This type of set-up works excellent with the combination of other equipment, such as medicine ball, bands and dumbbells. Any sequence is OK! No rules! However, try to balance the workout so that all body parts are hit from all angles – how you get that done is half the fun! Below is just one of many circuits you can create using the stability ball. You can fit one person per station and have them rotate in any direction.

Sample Stability Ball Circuit

This circuit allows 16 people to participate. You can rotate in any give direction and add other equipment to this configuration – your imagination is the only limitation to circuit design. You can even add or substitute some cardio equipment like bikes, treadmills or Versa climbers to really kick this training into another gear.

Bench Press	Supine rotations	Leg Curls	Band Rowing
Bridges	Wall Slide	Sitting balance	Shoulder press
Crunch	Prone Leg ext	Upright Rowing	Bear Balance
1 arm Rowing	One leg SB squat	Roller coaster	Skiers

This circuit can be flexible enough so that the participants can be of varying fitness levels – all you have to do is tweak the exercises to fit the individual at that station.

Integration into a traditional program

We have already talked about the 3TIS. Below is a sample of how stability ball training can fit into a traditional program.

SB training can be integrated into any training program.

One can follow the standard Periodization model set forth by Bompa, Stone, Kreamer and others. The SB exercises can follow the rep and set scheme of the Periodization cycle the client is currently in.

A 2 week micro cycle could look like the figure below:

▨ Traditional Strength Exercise   ☐ Complimentary stability ball Equivalent

Note: This is just a basic sample of a 2-week micro-cycle. The needs of every client are different. The needs analysis should include a functional evaluation and specific program design tailored to meet the goals of the individual.

Program notes and comments:

The reason we chose two weeks is because it provides every major muscle system three days of training stimuli through the standard modalities, as well as the functional modalities. This program would provide enough intensity and volume of traditional work to stimulate hypertrophy and absolute strength development. At the same time, 3 days of functional training for every major movement component and muscle system will surely put more "hustle behind all that muscle."

We have seen this program work very effectively with athletes and non-athletes alike. In our practice, we observe significant strength gains with this program, as expressed by standard lifts (e.g. squat, bench, etc.). However, we also find an concomitant increase in movement skill and balance.

We believe in this integrated method of training, especially if hypertrophy is a major issue. Many of our clients like the diversity of functional training with the SB so much, they never train on machines again. Therefore, we let the desires and the needs of the client dictate the ratio of integration using various modalities. Regardless, SB training is an incredible tool to incorporate into any training program. We use it and urge you to do the same.

Week 1

Body Part	Monday	Wednesday	Friday
Total Body Power	Power Cleans	Roller coasters	Box jumps
Legs/hips	Squats	SB One Leg Squats	Lateral Lunges
Back	Elbow SB rollouts	One Arm Row	One arm rows with SB stab
Chest	DB SB Bench press	Flat Bench	SB Push-ups
Shoulders	Standing DB Press	Alternating SB DB Laterals	Heavy DB Alternating Upright rows
Core/ Balance	Supine rotations	Weighted hypers Biofoam Putting	One leg Supine leg curl

Week 2

Body Part	Monday	Wednesday	Friday
Total Body Power	Explosive hypers On SB	Power Snatch	Impact lockouts
Legs/hips	One leg hip lifts	Squats	Lateral SB One-leg squats
Back	Cable Row	DB alternating pullovers	Pull-downs
Chest	Incline DB Bench	One arm DB bench -mobility	Flat Bench
Shoulders	One arms DB Snatch -sitting	Standing BB PBN	Alternating SB DB OH presses
Core/ Balance	Resisted Sit-up Airplane	Three point bear balance	Hanging Knee tucks Rocker board

Conclusion

Stability ball training is an effective and versatile method of improving performance. It is well tolerated by all populations and can be found in various settings. Although specific research is hard to come by, the body of work on postural stabilization and core development clearly demonstrates the efficacy of stability ball training.

Stabilization Limited Training may provide a piece of the puzzle that is "optimum performance". This method of training provides superior stabilization to the core as well as the extremities, while reducing the deficit between functional and absolute strength. The objective of SLT is to develop "strength one can use". SLT aids in this endeavor by re-educating the CNS and providing a more stable foundation from which force production can be initialized and transferred.

The strength of any training program does not reside on an exclusive approach to performance enhancement, but rather on an integrated model using a variety of modalities, which effectively targets the desired training adaptations. The 3 Tier Integrated System offers such a model. It offers three levels of integration, whereby the effectiveness of traditional training modalities can be augmented by new and revolutionary training methods. Stability ball training serves the 3TIS model by its adaptability and ease of use.

SB exercises have been taken to the next level. They are effective, practical and fun. The fitness professional's ability to explain the purpose of and incorporate this modality of exercises will certainly be one of the most useful tools in increasing and retaining a healthy, and high-performance client base.

Flexibility Exercises

Purpose:
The following SB stretches will provide proprioceptive flexibility. This is made possible by the SB's unstable nature. The speed of execution can range from slow and controlled to ballistic. Make sure that the ROM and speed of movement is appropriate for the client.

1) Posterior and Anterior Hip Tilts
Main Muscles Stretched: Abdominal and Low Back Musculature

Comments and Teaching Cues:
Posterior and anterior hip tilts prepares the neuromuscular system to start "tuning into the core" musculature

Sit up tall and keep the core tight.

Keep the shoulders stationary and just tilt the hip forward and backwards.

2) Lateral Hip Tilts
Main Muscles Stretched: Oblique Abdominals and Low Back Musculature

Comments and Teaching Cues:
Lateral hip tilts also focus on tuning into the core muscles.

Keep the shoulders leveled and roll the ball by tilting the hips laterally, not moving the entire body over the SB.

3) Hip circles (clock/counter)
Main Muscles Stretched: Abdominal and Low Back Musculature

Comments and Teaching Cues:
Hip circles bring the entire core musculature into action.

Sit up tall and keep the belly through the spine.

Keep shoulders at the center of the action while moving the hips in circular motion.

4) Lateral Adductor
Main Muscles Stretched: Hip Adductors

Comments and Teaching Cues:
The lateral adductor stretch further stretches the hips focusing on the adductor group

Sit up tall and keep the core tight.

Move the entire body over one leg. Push off with the trailing leg and straighten it out at the end of the movement..

5) Side Oblique to mobility oblique
    Main Muscles Stretched: Oblique Abdominal and Low Back Musculature

Comments and Teaching Cues:
    Side oblique stretches in this position contniue to strech the adductors while bringing in the obliques.
    At the top of the adductor stretch, laterally flex over the support leg – use arm for additional stretch of the core msucles.

6) Curl-up ➔ toe touch ➔ alt leg

Comments and Teaching Cues:
    Curl up and toe touches concentrate on lumbar, hamstrings and soleus flexibility.
    Curl up the body into a ball to stretch back and soleus and straighten legs to focus on hamstrings.

7) Split lunge hip flexor
Main Muscles Stretched: Hip Flexors

Comments and Teaching Cues:
The split lunge stretch hits the hip flexors of the trailing leg when upright and
The extensors of the front leg when flexing forward.
Support the longest stance possible, using the SB to support your body weight..
Bend over as far as you can go.
Bring your body back up to an upright position – then lean back as far as possible without feeling pressure in you lower back.

8) Supine abdominal / chest stretch
Main Muscles Stretched: Abdominal and Chest Muscles

Comments and Teaching Cues:
Great stretch for the abdominals and balance while in a supported position.
Gently roll back on ball raising the hips to expand the chest and abdominals.
Open your arms and let them fall back opening up and stretching the chest muscles.
You can increase the intensity by performing this stretch on a single leg.

9) Rotations→ mobility
Main Muscles Stretched: Obliques and Hip Flexors

Comments and Teaching Cues:
Keep hands in front of chest as you roll from shoulder to shoulder on the apex of the ball.

Very important to keep the hips elevated in order to create a stretch on the hip flexors, adductors and internal rotators.

10) Supine side to side lateral rolls
Main Muscles Stretched: Oblique abdominals and low back musculature

Comments and Teaching Cues:
This supine exercise warms up the scapular complex while addressing kenisthetics.

Maintain hip extension and body alignment in order to increase core and hip involvement.

Start with a mild roll while maintaining a horizontal orientation of the arms.

11) Prone spinal rolls
Main Muscles Stretched: Back Extensors

Comments and Teaching Cues:
The prone spinal roll is a gentle way of stretching the entire spine.
Allows the novice to get use to using the ball with this simple move.
Put your belly on the ball and simply roll back and forth while relaxing the spine muscles.

12) Kneeling hip flex/ext
Main Muscles Stretched: Both Hip Flexors and Extensors

Comments and Teaching Cues:
This is a more pronounced hip flexor stretch.
Notice the deeper split lunge position supported by the ball.
Kneel behind the ball, placing the ball up against your thigh.
Put your belly on the ball and relax.
You may want to use a pad under the knee supporting the body.
Extend back up to a straight position, then lean back without feeling pressure on the lower back.

13) Posterior Shoulder
Main Muscles Stretched: Posterior Shoulder and Scapular complex

Comments and Teaching Cues:
This posterior shoulder stretch hits the entire upper and middle back concentrating on rotational flexibility.

Kneel in front of the ball and cross your left arm leaning the elbow on the SB.

Roll the SB to your right until your rotation allows the back of your shoulder to touch the ball.

You may want to use a pad under the knees for support, especially on hard surfaces.

14) Prone Core Rocking
Main Muscles Stretched: Abdominals, Low back, and Hip Flexors

Comments and Teaching Cues:
Prone rocking is harder than it looks, it really warms up the core and hip flexors.
Use a small SB (e.g. 55 cm)
Put your chest on the SB, keep a posterior pelvic tilt and the lower body supported on the balls of the feet.
Hug the ball and keep the arms in touch with the SB at all times.
Rock from side to side, trying to touch your elbows to the floor.

 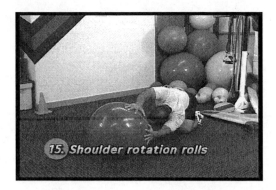

15) Shoulder rotation rolls
   Main Muscles Stretched: Shoulder Flexors and Oblique Abdominals

   Comments and Teaching Cues:
   Shoulder rollouts stretch out the shoulder complex along with the pulling muscles of the back. The additional rotation further stretches the obliques and other muscles of the core.
   Kneel down putting your hands on the SB.
   While sitting on your ankles, flex at the hips leaning your upper body forward.
   Roll the SB from side to side.
   Keep your core tight and cervical spine neutral.

Chest Exercises

Purpose:

The following SB exercises will enhance scapular stabilization while developing core strength, especially in the abdominal and hip flexor area. The chest musculature and a pushing motion will be emphasized. However, due to the SLT methodology that SB training is predicated on, exercise execution will greatly depend on stability not prime mover strength.

1) Protraction / retraction stabilization with two legs on ball

TEACHING CUES – Mounting (applies to all prone "hands of floor" exercises):

>*Get on knees in front of SB, laying your belly and chest on the SB.*
>
>*Roll over the SB and start walking with your hands as you extend your legs off the ground. Walk out as far as the exercise requires and your strength allows.*
>
>**Keep your body straight and tight –belly in!**

TEACHING CUES – Body alignment (applies to all prone exercises):

>*Best time to teach body alignment and proper core stabilization*
>
>*Keep core tight and "belly through the spine." NO pressure on the lower back!*
>
>*Do not allow the hips to rise or sag down to the ground!*
>
>*Keep straight body alignment – from head to toes.*
>
>Start teaching the progression with a posterior pelvic tilt and progress to a neutral spine as client develops core strength.
>
>The greater the distance between the ground support and ball support, the harder the exercise.

TEACHING CUES – retraction/protraction

>Retraction refers to the movement action not the concentric muscle action. Gravity is providing the retraction with the protractors decelerating the movement.
>
>Allow the scapular complex to relax into a retracted position. Look for wrinkle in back of shirt.
>
>Protract the scapular complex as to stretch the back of the shirt.

2) Protraction/retraction stabilization with one leg on ball

      TEACHING CUES:

> Start by walking out using two legs, then balancing on a single leg .
> Gradually work to a single leg walkout.
> Follow the upper progression of the two-leg version.
> Keep body straight and core tight.

3) Walk outs with two legs on ball

      TEACHING CUES:

> Walkout using small steps and gradually increase the steps.
> Start the progression with a wider foot base and gradually work the progression so that the knees and ankles are together.
> Keep the scapular complex stabilized – don't let the shirt wrinkle between the shoulder blade.
> This exercise trains the balance and strength needed to begin the push-up progression.

4) Walkouts with one leg on ball
    TEACHING CUES:

        Mount the ball and balance on a single leg.

        Take small steps with the arms and work to larger steps.

        Keep the hips leveled horizontally and don't let them rotate.

        Don't allow shoulder complex or hips to collapse.

5) Clock walks with two legs on ball
    TEACHING CUES:

        Mount the ball and balance on a single leg.

        Take small steps with the arms and work to larger steps.

        Walk out to appropriate distance.

        Take lateral steps as if you were a clock.

        Start going to 1 and back. Progress to 12 (i.e. 360 degrees)

        Keep the hips leveled horizontally and don't let them rotate.

        Don't allow shoulder complex or hips to collapse.

6) Push-up progression with two legs on ball
TEACHING CUES:

Push-ups can be varied in intensity by ball placement. The closer the ball is to the feet, the harder the exercise.

The three basic positions for ball support are Hips, Knees, and Feet.

Start with wide foot base and progress the legs closer together until the knees and ankle touch.

Follow all stabilization cues of the previous progressions.

7) Push-up progression with two leg toe balance
TEACHING CUES:

Walk out until nothing but the toes are supporting the lower body on the SB.

Start the push-up keeping the body straight and core tight.

This requires additional stability at the ankle complex.

8) Push-up progression with one leg on ball
   TEACHING CUES:

   Start the progression by walking out on two legs, then balancing on a single leg.

   Once balanced on a single leg, perform a push-up keeping the core tight and body perfectly aligned.

   Progress to a single leg walkout followed by the push-up.

   Utilize the lever system to adjust the exercise. Start with the SB under the thigh and work the progression to the knee, shin and foot.

9) Push-up progression with one leg toe balance
   TEACHING CUES:

   Start the progression by walking out on two legs, then balancing on a single leg.

   Once balanced on a single leg, perform a push-up keeping the core tight and body perfectly aligned.

   Progress to a single leg walkout followed by the push-up.

   Utilize the lever system to adjust the exercise. Start with the SB under the thigh and work the progression to the knee, shin, foot and finally to the ball of the foot.

76

10) Kneeling protraction hands on ball
TEACHING CUES:

The next step in the push-up progression is to start hand balancing on the ball.

Orient your hands slightly outward and place the ball so that the ball is directly under your chest and chin, not your head.

Keep perfect alignment from knees to head.

As with the push-ups, start with protraction lockouts supported on the knees.

You may want to use a pad under your knees for support.

11) Kneeling lockouts with hands on ball
TEACHING CUES:

Lockouts are partial push-ups. .

Keep hands oriented slightly out and perfect body alignment from knees to head.

Start the progression with the SB close to your thighs. As you get stronger, progress the SB out away from you.

Maintain good scapular stabilization and gradually increase the depth of the lock out. Eventually it becomes a push-up.

You may want to use a pad under your knees for support.

12) Kneeling pushups hands on ball
TEACHING CUES:

Perform these as you did the lockouts.

Continue to increase the flexion at the elbows until your chest touches the ball, then push-up and lockout.

Maintain good scapular stabilization and gradually increase the depth of the lockout. Eventually, it becomes a push-up.

You may want to use a pad under your knees for support.

13) Protraction/retraction stab. hands on ball, feet on floor
TEACHING CUES:

The first exercise in the advanced progression for the "hands on ball" push-up is scapular protraction.

It is acceptable to add a partial lockout as a "skill transfer" exercise.

Maintain good scapular stabilization and gradually increase the depth of the lockout. Eventually, it becomes a push-up.

Keep core tight and a perfect body alignment.

14) Pushup with hands on ball, feet on floor
TEACHING CUES:

The only difference between this push-up and the previous protraction lockout is the amplitude of the exercise.

Lower the chest until it touches the ball, then press and lockout.

Keep hands oriented slightly out and lower the body slowly while keeping perfect alignment.

15) Pushups with two hands on ball, feet elevated
TEACHING CUES:

To increase the intensity to the push-up progression, elevate the feet.

This puts more weight on the arms and increases the stability demands as well as core strength.

Keep a posterior pelvic tilt and keep the scapulas from collapsing to a retracted position.

Start with lockout and progress to full range push-ups.

16) Push-ups with one hand on ball, feet on floor
  TEACHING CUES:

> For the ultimate in shoulder and core stability, try the one arm push-up on the ball.
>
> This exercise reigns supreme in shoulder and core stability.
>
> Maintain a wide stance to provide an adequate balance base.

NOTE: At the time of the ESBT video release we did not have an "intermediate" progression to assist us in teaching the one arm push-up. However, since the release of our videos, we have developed a great intermediate progression to help you learn the one SB arm push-up. It's called the **Lateral-Rocking push-up**.

Lateral-Rocking push-up
  TEACHING CUES:

> Get into a lock out position.
>
> Begin a push-up as you roll the SB to the left side. Lower your body on the left side of the ball (see above).
>
> All of the weight should be supported on the right side of the body and the body should be leveled and straight.
>
> Alternate the pattern to the right and left.

80

17) Hops

TEACHING CUES:

Once the proper strength base has been developed, performing hops are an excellent exercise to develop upper body power.

Do not perform this exercise before mastering all previous exercises in the push-up progression. The deceleration shocks can hyperextend the back or cause injury to an unstable shoulder.

Balance on the SB while being supported under the hips.

Hop with your arms until the ball is under the feet. Hop back until the SB is under the hips again.

18) Clock hops

TEACHING CUES:

Clock hops add a nice lateral component to the upper body explosiveness developed by the hops.

Master all previous progressions prior to attempting this exercise and maintain proper alignment and shoulder stability.

Get out into a "feet on SB" position. Grab the ball with your feet.

Start hopping laterally. Go from 12 o'clock to 3 o'clock then back to 12. Gradually work to a 360 degree clock hop.

Keep volume low to avoid wrist and shoulder "over use" injuries.

19) Push-ups with two hands on two balls
TEACHING CUES:

Variations of the push-up can be performed by bringing in another ball.

Start with identical balls and proceed to different size balls with different inflation pressure.

Follow the same progression as the "hands on ball" progression.

Allow the SBs to touch for additional stability. Keep the SBs apart for additional balance and stability demands.

20) Pec-deck using two balls with feet on floor
TEACHING CUES:

With a little imagination any machine exercise can be duplicated with the SB.

The Peck Deck move can be performed using two SBs.

Different sizes and inflation pressures can add to the diversity of application.

Balance on the elbows keeping perfect body alignment.

Roll the SBs out until the chest is even with the SBs.

Bring the elbows close to each other without letting the SBs touch.

21) Big ball push-up
TEACHING CUES:

Push-ups can also be performed on large balls.

Since they elevate the feet, more weight can be transferred to the arms. This increases the intensity of this exercise.

Follow the same progressions you used for the other "feet on SB" push-ups (i.e. exercises 13-15)

CHEST - EXTERNAL RESISTANCE

The external resistance progressions for all body-parts are the same. They follow a logical order, which is simple and easy to remember. When working with dumbbells, perform the pressing or pulling motions in the following order:

1. Simultaneous movement pattern
2. Alternating movement pattern
3. Alternating with mobility (i.e. rocking from side to side at the end of a movement)
4. One arm
5. One arm with mobility

The following chest pressing exercises will illustrate this progression. However, all pressing and pulling movements will use this progression. Therefore, learn it and use it. Your client's safety and success may depend on it.

MOUNTING (same for all supine pressing exercises):
> Sit on the ball and put the DBs on the thighs.
> Lean back as your feet walk out.
> Keep the DBs at the chest while your walking out.
> Walk out until the SB is between the shoulder blades.
> Keep the hips up for the flat bench and allow them to drop for the incline version.
> Balance yourself on the SB before you start to press.
> Keep the spine neutral from hip to head
> Keep belly through the spine, look at the ceiling.

22) Dumbbell flat bench two arms simultaneous
> **TEACHING CUES:**
>> First, in the external resistance progression, is simultaneous pressing.
>> This allows one to learn the balance aspect of the pressing exercises while balancing on the ball.
>> Mount the ball and balance.
>> Press the DBs in a simultaneous fashion as you would in a DB bench press.
>> Make sure the lockout lines up the wrist elbow and shoulder.

23) Dumbbell flat bench two arms alternating
TEACHING CUES:

Alternating pressing teaches an individual unilateral movement and while adjusting their balance to a changing center of gravity.

Mount the ball and balance.

Press one DB while holding the other outside your chest.

Start the progression by pressing one DB at a time in an alternating fashion.

Progress to - As the pressed DB comes down, begin to press the other. This adds stabilization and balance demands.

Start with a narrow DB path and work your way to a wider pressing position. This increases the lever arm of this exercise for added difficulty.

24) Dumbbell flat bench one arm pressing
TEACHING CUES:

One arm pressing teaches unilateral loading and the additional stabilization requirement associated with this type of loading pattern.

Mount and balance on the ball.

Press the DB to a lockout position.

Again, start with the DB close to the body and then work to a wider position.

85

25) **Dumbbell flat bench one arm pressing with mobility**
   TEACHING CUES:
   Mount and balance on the ball.
   Press the DB to a lockout position as you rotate your shoulder blade off the SB.
   Again, start with the DB close to the body and then work to a wider position.
   Make sure the hips are kept at shoulder level.
   Keep the core tight throughout movement.

26) **Powerball flat bench two arm pressing**
   TEACHING CUES:
   Power Balls can be also used for pressing.
   Holding and balancing these balls adds an additional demand for control and stability.
   Mount the ball and balance.
   Press the Power balls in a simultaneous fashion as you would in a DB bench press.
   Make sure the lockout lines up the wrist elbow and shoulder.

27) Powerball flat bench alternating and one arm pressing (picture not shown)
   TEACHING CUES:

Unilaterally loading the exercise using one Powerball will challenge the demands of core stabilization.

Begin with the Powerball or resistance close to the midline of the body and progress in difficulty by bringing the Powerball farther away through the motion of the exercise.

Add mobility for additional balance demands.

28) Dumbbell flat bench fly two arms simultaneous
   TEACHING CUES:

Performing flys on the SB adds a whole new dimension to this standard exercise.

Mount and balance on the ball.

Press the DB to a lockout position then lower the DBs into a fly position (shown above)

Keep the hips up and the core tight.

29) Dumbbell flat bench fly two arms alternating
   TEACHING CUES:

Alternating patterns in this exercise add balance demands.

Mount and balance on the ball. Press the DBs to a lockout position then lower the left arm as shown in the picture.

Bring the left arm up as the right arm goes down.

Keep the hips up and stable – keep the core tight!

30) Dumbbell flat bench fly one arm
TEACHING CUES:

Performing one arm flys on the SB really increases the stabilization requirements.

Mount and balance on the ball.

Press the DB to a lockout position.

Perform a fly as shown above.

Keep the hips up and the core tight.

31) Dumbbell flat bench fly one arm with mobility
TEACHING CUES:

Adding mobility to this exercise further increases the stabilization requirements.

Mount and balance on the ball.

Press the DB to a lockout position.

Perform a fly, as shown above, with mobility (i.e. let the shoulder blades comes off the SB when you rotate).

Keep the hips up and the core tight.

32) Dumbbell incline bench two arms simultaneous
    TEACHING CUES:

> This inclined position increases the involvement of the shoulders over the chest and triceps.
>
> The same progression previously discussed for the flat bench applies to the incline bench press. However, the hips are allowed to drop below the shoulder line to create the incline position.
>
> Mount and balance on the SB.
>
> 2 Arm pressing is always the first in the progression

33) Dumbbell incline bench two arms alternating
    TEACHING CUES:

> 2 Arm alternation work is the next step in progression
>
> First use a narrow path, then open up the arms to create greater torque at the shoulder joint.
>
> Mount and balance on the ball allowing hips to drop below the shoulder line to create the incline position.
>
> Press one DB up and keep the other at the shoulder line.
>
> Alternate presses.

34) Dumbbell incline bench one arm pressing
   TEACHING CUES:

> Single arm work is the next step in progression and by far the most challenging of the presses from a stability viewpoint.
>
> First, use a narrow path. Then open up the arm to create greater torque at the shoulder joint.
>
> Mount and balance on the ball allowing hips to drop below the shoulder line to create the incline position.
>
> Press the DB up.
>
> Keep the core tight and cervical spine neutral.

35) Dumbbell incline bench one arm pressing with mobility
   TEACHING CUES:

> Finally, we add some mobility to the 1 Arm press for additional balance requirement and core involvement.
>
> Mount and balance on the ball.
>
> Press the DB to a lockout position as you rotate your shoulder blade off the SB.
>
> Again, start with the DB close to the body and then work to a wider position.
>
> Keep the core tight throughout movement.

36. Powerball incline bench two arms simultaneous

36) Power ball incline bench two arms simultaneous
TEACHING CUES:

Again, the Power balls add a different angle and demand to any exercise.

Using two balls of different weights creates a challenging movement out of the simplest of exercises.

The same progression previously discussed for the incline bench applies.

Mount and balance on the SB.

2-arm simultaneous pressing is always the first in the progression.

Move from a narrow to a wider pattern for increased difficulty.

37. Dumbbell incline bench fly two arms simultaneous

37) Dumbbell incline fly two arms simultaneous
TEACHING CUES:

The incline fly can follow the same progression as the fly progression in the flat position exercises.

Mount and balance on the SB.

2-arm simultaneous movement is always the first in the progression.

38. Dumbbell incline bench fly
two arms alternating

38) Dumbbell incline fly two arms alternating
   TEACHING CUES:

   Alternating this exercise really challenges the stability of the core and shoulder joint complex.

   Try to emphasize smooth movement and maintain a 90-degree position of alternating arms.

   Mount and balance on the ball keeping your hips low. Press the DBs to a lockout position then lower the right arm as shown in the picture above.

   Bring the left arm up as the right arm goes down.

   Keep the hips stable and the core tight!

39) Dumbbell complex chest fly/pullover/flat bench
TEACHING CUES:

For exhaustive circuit style work, one can certainly link various exercises together.

Here, a Chest Fly, Pull-over and a Flat Bench are linked to form a Push/Pull circuit.

Your goals and imagination will dictate what circuits you create.

Perform complex in sequence or succession.

Follow the teaching dues discussed for each exercise.

40) Dumbbell complex chest & shoulders overhead press/ incline bench/ flat bench
   TEACHING CUES:

Complexes can also follow a pre-exhaustion succession.

This complex takes you from the weakest mechanical position, being the shoulder press, to the strongest mechanical position being the chest press.

Follow the cues as described in this manual and the videos for each exercise.

Shoulder Exercises

Purpose:

The following SB exercises will enhance stabilization in the shoulder complex while developing core strength and balance. The shoulder musculature and a pushing motion will be emphasized. However, due to the SLT methodology that SB training is predicated on, exercise execution will greatly depend on stability not prime mover strength.

MOUNTING THE BALL (applies to all tuck presses):

Get on your knees and put your belly on the ball.

Walk the hands forward and straighten out your legs to balance as you would when performing a "hands on floor" push-up.

Walk out till the knees are on the ball.

1) Knee tuck press
TEACHING CUES:

The knee tuck press allows an individual to perform an overhead press with a small fraction of their body weight.

The percentage of the body weight that is applied to the exercise is dependent on tuck position, size of ball, and angle of pressing.

Mount the SB.

Tuck your knees and balance.

Perform a hand press.

Allow the ball to roll back and forth as you press.

2) Big ball knee tuck press
TEACHING CUES:

A large ball can be used to modify the angle of pressing so that the shoulder press movement is emphasized.

This position provides a more vertical orientation; therefore, more body weight is placed on the shoulders increasing resistance.

Follow the same cues as the small SB tuck press.

3) Pike press
TEACHING CUES:

Next on the shoulder progression is the pike press. This not only requires exceptional shoulder strength but extraordinary core strength and hamstring flexibility.

The tighter the pike tuck the more weight is placed on the shoulders and arms.

There is no way to become proficient at this exercise unless you have total mastery over the previous tucked presses.

Mount the SB.

Flex you hips, keeping your legs straight (i.e. pike tuck) and balance on your toes.

Perform a hand press.

The ball should not balance.

4) Big ball pike press
TEACHING CUES:

The big ball shoulder press requires superior upper-body strength because it facilitates a more vertical position.

Follow the same cues as the small SB pike tuck press.

5) One leg pike press
TEACHING CUES:

One leg support work complicates the pike press.

The vertical leg really adds additional weight, balance and stabilization requirements to this exercise.

The smaller SB requires more flexibility but less strength.

Follow the cues for the two-leg pike press.

Lift one leg and perform a hand press.

6) **Big Ball, one leg shoulder pike press**
   TEACHING CUES:

   The larger ball increases the resistance at the expense of flexibility and core strength demands. The larger SB requires less flexibility but more strength.

   Strong individuals with limited flexibility will find this version of the 1 Leg shoulder press more suitable.

   Follow the cues for the two-leg pike press.

   Lift one leg and perform a hand press.

7) **Roller coaster**
   TEACHING CUES:

   After developing the proper shoulder strength, one can perform explosive exercises to help develop shoulder power.

   The roller coaster is fun, safe and really accentuates shoulder explosiveness.

   Sit on top of a small SB while situating another one in front of you.

   Launch your body forward and roll over the SB that is in front of you.

   Hold the SB you are sitting on with your legs.

   Land on you hands

8) Big ball Roller Coaster
TEACHING CUES:

The Large Ball Roller Coaster adds a different dimension and angle of attack. It puts more weight on the shoulders, thus, increases the demands for strength.

Put your chest on the ball and balance.

Push-off with your feet, propelling your body forward.

Roll over the SB and land on your hands, out and away from the SB.

Decelerate your body with your arms and quickly push back.

Try to get your body back behind the SB with one quick and solid push. Minimize the amount of hand/ground contact time.

Work the landing out further from the SB for added intensity.

9) **Shoulder complex 1, reverse hyper / press**
    TEACHING CUES:

> Body weight complexes can be tailored to any situation.
> Here, a simple shoulder press is linked to a reverse hyper.
> Lay over the SB so that your hands are on the ground and the hips are flexed.
> Perform a reverse hyper and hold the extended position.
> Perform a press.
> Perform a reverse hyper after the press.
> Repeat the sequence.

100

10) Shoulder complex 2, pushup / tuck press /pike press / one leg press
   TEACHING CUES:

As we previously showed you in the chest DB complexes, we can use a body weight circuit that takes you from the strongest mechanical position to the weakest lifting position.

This is similar to a pyramid-loading scheme.

Mount the large SB and walk out till the knees are above the SB.

Flex the hips to get into a pike position and perform a handstand.

Extend the body and perform a push-up.

Tuck the body and perform a tuck press.

SHOULDERS - EXTERNAL RESISTANCE

11) **Dumbbell sitting overhead press two arms simultaneous**
   TEACHING CUES:

   The same progression we used in the chest – external resistance exercises apply to the shoulders.

   Sitting on the Stability Ball requires an enormous amount of core stability, balance and shoulder flexibility. To properly execute this exercise you also need good shoulder flexibility.

   Sit and balance on the SB.

   For lighter weights, bend over, grab the DBs and pull them to the shoulders. Press the DBs overhead to a lockout position over the shoulders.

   For heavier weights, use a spotter to hand you the weight and spot you during the press.

   Do not lean back to finish the press. Sit up straight with your center of mass between your feet and the top of the ball.

12) **Dumbbell sitting overhead press two arms alternating with mobility**
   TEACHING CUES:

   Less shoulder flexibility is required for alternating presses, but the moving center of mass caused by the alternating pattern requires greater balance and core strength.

   Follow the cues for the simultaneous pressing. Alternate pressing patterns. Add some core lateral flexion to add mobility and intensity.

13) Dumbbell sitting overhead press one arm pressing
   TEACHING CUES:

> Single Arm pressing puts a great deal of contra-lateral stability demand on the core.
>
> Sit on SB and balance.
>
> Pick up DB with both hands and balance at one shoulder.
>
> Press the DB overhead with one arm.
>
> Keep core tight and body straight.

14) Dumbbell sitting overhead press with two arms pressing with mobility
   TEACHING CUES:

> Mobility can later be added to one arm presses to increase the neural demand.
>
> Sit on SB and balance.
>
> Pick up DB with both hands and balance at one shoulder.
>
> Press the DB overhead with one arm while elevating the shoulder and translating your weight to one hip.
>
> Keep core tight and body straight.

15) Power ball sitting overhead press with two arms simultaneous
TEACHING CUES:

This two-arm press is hard enough without the varying weight of the Power Ball. Add asymmetrical loading to create additional stabilization requirements.

Sit on the SB and balance.

Follow the same progression, as indicated, for the sitting overhead presses with DBs.

16) Power ball sitting overhead press with one arm
TEACHING CUES:

Power balls can be brought in the overhead press.

Using asymmetrical loading further challenges the neuromuscular system due to increased stability and balance demands.

The progression is consistent as with the other exercise

17) Dumbbell sitting lateral raise two arms simultaneous
   TEACHING CUES:

   Standard exercises, like laterals, can be made more challenging by performing them while sitting on a SB.

   Sit on the SB and balance.

   Pick up the DBs and let them hang at your side. Raise them to the side slowly.

   Add asymmetrical loading to create additional stabilization requirements.

   You can also try performing this exercise while supporting the sitting position with only one leg.

18) Dumbbell sitting lateral raise two arms alternating
   TEACHING CUES:

   Alternating the lateral raise pattern moves the body's center of mass in the frontal plane. This kicks up the balance and stability demands.

   Sit on the SB and balance.

   Pick up the DBs and let them hang at your side. Raise one of them while leaving the other at your side.

   Add asymmetrical loading to create additional stabilization requirements.

   You can also try performing this exercise while supporting the sitting position with only one leg.

19) Dumbbell sitting lateral raise two arms alternating with mobility
TEACHING CUES:

Alternating patterns add a whole new look, and feel, to the shoulder lateral exercise especially when mobility is added.

Pick up the DBs and let them hang at your side. Raise one of them while leaving the other at your side. Slightly rock your hips to the side of the raised DB. Keep the stance wide.

Sit on the SB and balance.

Add asymmetrical loading to create additional stabilization requirements.

You can also try performing this exercise while supporting the sitting position with only one leg.

20) Dumbbell sitting lateral raise with one arm
TEACHING CUES:

As usual, one arm work allows unilateral loading, shifting the center of mass and increasing the need for balance and stability.

Sit on the SB and balance.

Pick up the DB and let it hang at your side. Raise it to the side slowly.

Add mobility and single leg support for additional balance and stability demands.

21) Dumbbell sitting front raise with one arm
TEACHING CUES:

Again, as usual, one arm work allows unilateral loading. The front raise shifts the center of mass along the sagittal plane and the unilateral loading still challenges frontal plane stability.

Sit on the SB and balance.

Pick up the DB and let it hang at your side. Raise it to the front slowly.

Add mobility and single leg support for additional balance and stability demands.

22) Dumbbell sitting front/lateral raise combination
TEACHING CUES:

Here is a fun way to perform laterals. It challenges the frontal and sagittal planes of motion in an alternating and simultaneous fashion.

Sit on the SB and balance.

Pick up the DBs and hold them at your side. Raise one of them to the front while raising the other to the side. Bring them down and alternate the pattern.

Add asymmetrical loading to create additional stabilization requirements.

You can also try performing this exercise while supporting the sitting position with only one leg.

23) Power ball sitting lateral raise two arms simultaneous
TEACHING CUES:

Adding the gripping requirements of the Power ball brings in an additional component especially if asymmetrically loaded.

Follow the same cues you did for the DB version.

24) Dumbbell sitting upright rows two arms alternating
TEACHING CUES:

Upright rows can be performed from this sitting position using an alternating sequence.

With the dumbbell placement inside the knees, an additional rotational component is imposed on the core.

Sit on the SB and balance. Assume a wide support base with the feet.

Hold the DBs between your feet and perform alternating upright rows.

Make sure the core is kept tide by keeping the belly through the spine, especially if using a functional kyphotic position. Keep the weight light for this application.

Make sure the back is stabilized in a lordotic position when using aggressive loads.

25) Dumbbell sitting upright rows two arms alternating outside
TEACHING CUES:

Rowing to the outside of the knees increases the moment arm of this exercise. This emphasizes the upper back and posterior aspect of the shoulder.

The core is still engaged to stabilize and rotate.

Sit on the SB and balance. Assume a narrow support base with the feet.

Hold the DBs outside your feet and perform alternating upright rows.

Make sure the core is kept tide by keeping the belly through the spine,. especially if using a functional kyphotic position. Keep the weight light for this application.

Make sure the back is stabilized in a lordotic position when using aggressive loads.

26) Dumbbell sitting upright rows one arm inside
TEACHING CUES:

One arm rowing allows increased rotational mobility and increased core rotational demands.

Sit on the SB and balance. Assume a wide support base with the feet.

Hold the DB inside your feet and perform one-arm upright rows.

Keep the core tight.

Add rotation for additional core and balance demands

27) Dumbbell snatches
TEACHING CUES:

DB snatches provide a stabilization-limited modality to practice upper body explosive training. Great for individuals that are rehabbing a lower extremity injury where the standing position is contra-indicated.

If aggressive loads are going to be used, DBs offer better gripping and balance.

Sit on the SB and balance. Assume a wide support base with the feet.

Hold the DB inside your feet.

Pull the DB as if you were starting a lawn mower, using a high elbow pull.

Allow the DB to continue to move up to a lockout position over the shoulder.

Make sure the core is kept tide by keeping the belly through the spine – especially during the fast pulling motion.

Keep the weight light for this application.

Make sure the back is stabilized in a lordotic position when using aggressive loads

28) Power ball snatches
TEACHING CUES:

The purpose of illustrating this exercise is to show the diversity of implements you can use with the SB – "think outside the box!"

Use the same cues as #27.

29) Converta-ball snatches
TEACHING CUES:

Converta-balls also compliment SB training.

This type of ball uses a rope attachment making it more challenging on the wrist during deceleration.

Use the same cues as #27, gripping the ball by the rope.

30) Power ball clean & press with asymmetrical loading
TEACHING CUES:

Seated Cleans and Presses can be a real challenge with unevenly loaded Power balls. This is a fun application – don't take it too seriously!

With these exercises, balancing while performing presses, present the greatest challenge.

One-foot support further adds to the complexity of this exercise.

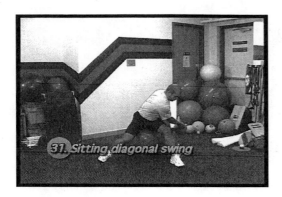 

31) Sitting diagonal swing
TEACHING CUES:

Rotational exercises, such as these swings, allow excellent work for accelerators and decelerators of the arm while still addressing core stabilization. The swinging nature of this exercise allows a considerable eccentric loading phase.

This type of exercise is very effective for conditioning throwing and racquet sport mechanics.

Here, a Converta-Ball is used. However, Power Balls or other implements could also be utilized.

Sit on SB, using a wide foot base, and attach the Coverta-ball to one hand via the rope.

Swing in a diagonal fashion, allowing upper body rotation.

Keep the core tight and stable.

32) Sitting side swings
TEACHING CUES:

Side swings are excellent for conditioning explosive rotational mechanics. The forehand or backhand versions can be performed, allowing an individual to concentrate on unilateral development.

Sit on SB, using a wide foot base, and attach the Coverta-ball to one hand and use a golfer's grip on the rope.

Swing in a horizontal fashion, allowing upper body rotation.

Keep the core tight and stable.

112

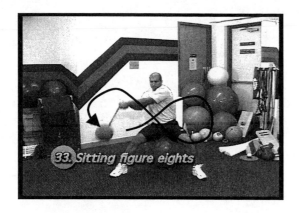

33) Sitting figure eights
TEACHING CUES:

Figure-eights provide enormous wrist, shoulder and core work.

The use of the Coverta-Ball is recommended due to the rope attachment. The additional length of the rope significantly increases the demand on wrists, shoulders and core –even in the sitting position.

Sit on SB, using a wide foot base, and attach the Coverta-Ball to one hand and use a golfer's grip on the rope.

Swing in a figure eight pattern, allowing some upper body movement.

Keep the core tight and stable.

34) Rotator cuff
TEACHING CUES:

Although we rarely use this type of isolation exercise, rotator cuff exercises can be performed while involved in "active sitting" on the SB.

This application is used to illustrate the diversity and integration capability of the SB into traditional training models.

Back Exercises

Purpose:

The following exercises are designed to strengthen the back and shoulder musculature. In contrast to the traditional exercises for the pulling muscle muscles, such as the pull-up, the SB exercises will mostly be limited by the core musculature. The Stabilization Limited Training environment of the SB requires the body to maintain specific positions that are in many cases extreme (e.g. roll-out progression) for successful execution. This chapter provides many exercises that exemplify the phrase – "training from the inside out."

1) Y's

> **TEACHING CUES: Mounting and stabilization position for Y T and Is.**
>> Kneel in front of the SB.
>> Secure the SB between the thigh and torso.
>> Lean your trunk on the ball, keeping the spine straight from hip to head.
>> Hold your scapulae in a depressed and retracted position during arm movements.

> **TEACHING CUES:**
>> Y's effectively target the scapular retractors and external rotators of the shoulder. Usually, body weight is sufficient resistance for most individuals. It targets the upper back and posterior deltoid while adding a nice balance component.
>> This exercise was used in the warm-up to prepare the upper back for work.
>> Place arms in a Y position with shoulders stabilized, and thumbs pointing to the ceiling.
>> Raise the arms as far as they will without compromising the stabilization of the spine and shoulders.
>> Once shoulder stabilization is learned, spinal flexion/extension and arm add/abduction can be incorporated into this exercise.

114

2) T's

TEACHING CUES:

> T's are a different version of the Y's. This focuses on scapular stabilization during movement when arms are abducted at 90-degrees
> Place the arms in the form of a T.
> Follow the identical progression outlined for the Ys

3) I's

TEACHING CUES:

> The exercise addresses the same retraction and external rotation components as the Ys and Ts.
> All three versions of this exercise can be performed in circuit fashion.
> They make an excellent warm-up to shoulder work or to balance out heavy chest work which facilitates protraction and internal rotation.
> Follow the same cues outlined for Ys

4) Supine side to side roll
 TEACHING CUES:

> This exercise was used in the warm-up to prepare the upper back for work. It targets the upper back and posterior deltoid while adding a nice balance component.
> Sit on the SB and balance.
> Walk your feet out and roll on the ball balancing the SB between your shoulder blades.
> Keep the hips leveled with the shoulders and the arms in a T position.
> Roll from side to side without changing the position of the shoulders or arms. The greater the roll, the greater the need for balance and posterior shoulder strength.
> Keep the core tight and hips high. Keep your eyes on the ceiling and cervical spine neutral.

5) Big ball supine side to side roll
 TEACHING CUES:

> Large balls can be used for these side rolls.
> Follow the same cues outlined for #4

Supplemental material

The rollout progression is a very advanced progression, even from the knees. Since the release of ESBT videos, we developed a new method of progressing beginners through this very difficult maneuver. This new version of the rollout allows everyone to enjoy this exercise in a safe and effective manner.

The adjustment we made is extremely simple – we use a wall to elevate the ball. This allows a very good range of motion and can be adjust from very light to intermediate work.

Straight arm shoulder rollout on wall
TEACHING CUES:

The wall rollout provides an excellent method of training the ventral musculature to decelerate shoulder flexion and spinal extension.

The wall support allows everyone, even geriatrics, to participate in this advanced progression.

Put ball at shoulder height and balance in a push-up position with the arms locked out.

Roll our hands and arms over the ball till your body is fully extended.

Keep the core tight and belly through the spine.

Move your feet back and ball down to increase the resistance of this exercise.

As with the other rollouts – **AVOID PRESSURE IN THE LOWER BACK.** If this happens, you have lost the stabilization war in the pelvic area – stop and back off the progression (i.e. bring feet closer to the wall and the ball up higher).

6) Elbow shoulder rollout from knees, hands together

Note for Rollout progression:

The entire rollout progression can be performed standing with the SB against the wall.

Rolling-out the SB on the wall allows anyone to use this advanced exercise progression.

Do not allow the hips to sag. Avoid pressure in the lumbar spine.

TEACHING CUES:

Rollouts are an aggressive progression for the prime movers involved in shoulder extension. The first exercise in the progression uses an elbow balance and closed hand position for the upper body support. Balancing on the knees also creates a shorter moment arm.

Balance on the knees in front of the SB.

Put your elbows at the top of the ball in such a way that a line can intersect your shoulders, hips and knees.

Keep your core tight and belly in as you roll your elbows out to an extended position.

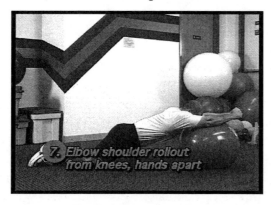

7) Elbow shoulder rollout from knees, hands apart
   TEACHING CUES:

When the hands are separated, additional strength and stabilization at the shoulders are required. Start with partial movement and slowly increase the range of motion as permitted by core stability.

Follow the same cues outlined in #6.

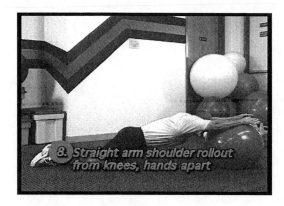

8) Straight arm shoulder rollout from knees, hands apart
TEACHING CUES:

Once the rollouts from the elbows have been mastered, straight-arm rollouts can be attempted. The longer moment arm provided by the straight-arm position really increases the intensity of this exercise.

Proper lower abdominal strength becomes increasingly important to protect the lower back.

Follow the same cues outline in #6.

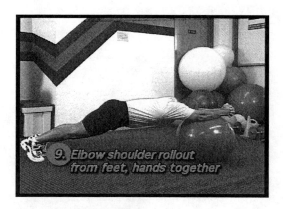

9) Elbow shoulder rollout from feet, hands apart
TEACHING CUES:

Elbow rollouts can now progress to balancing the lower body on the feet instead of the knees.

Even using the elbow rollout, the foot support creates a longer moment arm at the hips and shoulder, further increasing the core stabilization and upper body strength requirements.

Balance on both feet with your elbows on the SB. A line should intersect your shoulders, hips and ankles.

Keep your core tight and belly in as you roll your elbows out to an extended position.

No pressure should be felt in the lumbar spine. If you do – your abdominals and hip flexors have lost the stabilization war! This progression is too advanced for you go back to the knee support.

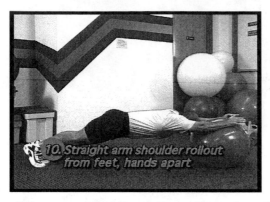

10) Straight arm shoulder rollout from feet, hands apart
TEACHING CUES:

The ultimate in core and shoulder extension training are these Straight arm Shoulder rollouts from the feet. This is an advanced exercise that should not be attempted by anyone who has not successfully progressed through the entire rollout progression.

Balance in a push-up position with the arms locked out.

Roll out hands and arms over the ball till your body is fully extended.

Follow all of the cues and precautions for #6-9.

 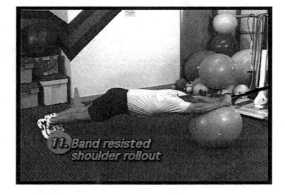

11) Band resisted shoulder rollout
TEACHING CUES:

The only exercise more challenging than a straight-arm, shoulder rollout from feet, is this exercise with external resistance.

Here, a band is used to add the resistance.

This exercise is only suitable for elite level training and not necessary for most individuals.

Follow all of the cues and precautions outlined for #6-10.

12) Band resisted compound rollout
TEACHING CUES:

This rollout uses a combination of hip and shoulder action. That is, a combination of hip flexion, as well as shoulder extension. Again, the external resistance is provided by a rubber band.

Kneel in front of the SB, balancing your forearms on the SB while holding on to the bands.

Flex the hips so that your upper body is parallel to the floor.

Perform a row/pull as you roll your arms over the ball.

13) Seated rowing standard
TEACHING CUES:

Rowing with the arms in a neutral position allows one to bring in the major muscle of the back, allowing more weight to be used.

Place the ball on the ground behind you. Grab the bands and pull back to sit on the ball.

Sit on the SB while holding on to the band. Keep you chest out and belly in. Shoulder blades down.

Perform a row with a neutral arm position.

Go to a single leg balance for additional stabilization and balance demands.

14) Seated rowing high
TEACHING CUES:

High arm rowing places more demand on the upper back and posterior portion of the shoulders.

Follow the cues for #13.

Perform a row with a high arm position.

15) Seated rowing compound
TEACHING CUES:

Due to larger muscle mass being used, larger loads can be implemented. Try doing all three variations of the seated row with single arm and diagonal patterns for added core stabilization requirements.

Follow the cues for #13-14.

Perform a row with a neutral arm position. Allow the upper body to reach forward when extending the arm.

Come back to an upright position with a rowing motion.

16) Dumbbell row, chest on ball two arms simultaneous
   TEACHING CUES:

Two arm DB rowing while using the Stability Ball really puts an emphasis on the posterior aspect of the shoulder.

The knees, or balls of the feet, can support the lower-body.

Balance on the SB with your chest at the top of the ball.

Hold the DBs at the side of the SB then simultaneously pull the DBs up in a rowing motion.

Keep the core tight and cervical spine in neutral during the exercise.

17) Dumbbell row, chest on ball two arms alternating
   TEACHING CUES:

This alternating pattern really increases the need for core stability.

The knees, or balls of the feet, can support the lower-body.

Balance on the SB with your chest at the top of the ball.

Hold the DBs at the side of the SBen pull one DB up in a rowing motion while keeping the other DB down. Then perform an alternating rowing pattern.

Keep the core tight and cervical spine in neutral during the exercise.

18) Dumbbell row, chest on ball one arm
TEACHING CUES:

The single arm version allows great rotation, really bringing in the core musculature.

The knees, or balls of the feet can support the lower-body.

Balance on the SB with your chest at the top of the ball.

Hold one DB at the side of the SB and hold on to the SB with the other arm then pull the DB up in a rowing motion.

Keep the core tight and cervical spine in neutral during the exercise.

19) Dumbbell row, chest ball on one arm with mobility
TEACHING CUES:

Adding mobility creates greater core strength as well as stabilization.

The knees, or balls of the feet can support the lower-body.

Balance on the SB with your chest at the top of the ball.

Hold the DBs at the side of the SB. Pull the DBs up in a rowing motion with a rotational motion at the end of the pull.

Keep the core tight and cervical spine in neutral during the exercise.

20) Dumbbell row with one arm feet parallel
TEACHING CUES:

Single arm rowing can also be performed from a standing position with the support arm balancing the body on the ball. Use a triangular base between the hand and both feet for support.

Stand in a parallel stance with one hand on top of the SB.

Hold the DB with the free hand and allow the DB to hang directly below the shoulder.

Perform a one arm row and lean on the SB for support.

21) Dumbbell row with one-arm feet staggered
TEACHING CUES:

Various staggered foot positions can be utilized to change the stabilization requirements of the exercise.

Follow upper body cues outlined in #20.

Use a staggered foot position for support.

Keep the belly through the spine.

125

22) Dumbbell row with one arm feet further back
TEACHING CUES:

The greater the distance between the ball and the feet the harder the exercise balance becomes.

Follow the cues and recommendations for #20-21.

23) Dumbbell pullover two arms simultaneous
TEACHING CUES:

Pullovers can be performed on the SB to add a new dimension to this traditional exercise.

24) Dumbbell pullover two arms alternating
TEACHING CUES:

This exercise can also be executed in a two arm alternating sequence or with single arm.

Sit on the ball and put the DBs on the thighs. Lean back as your feet walk out. Keep the DBs at the chest while your walking out.

Walk out until the SB is between the scapulae, keeping the hips up.

Keep the spine neutral from hip to head. Maintain a tight core and look at the ceiling.

Allow one DB to go behind the head, keeping the other at the chest.

Perform alternating pullovers.

25) Power ball pullover two-arm simultaneous
TEACHING CUES:

For additional gripping and balancing demands, power balls can be used.

Use positioning cues outlined in #25.

Allow both power balls to go behind the head.

Perform a pullover simultaneously with both arms.

26) Power ball pullover two arms alternating
TEACHING CUES:

Alternating arms adds greater intensity.

Sit on the ball and put the power balls on the thighs. Lean back as your feet walk out. Keep the power balls at the chest while your walking out.

Sit on the SB and put the power balls on the thighs. Lean back as your feet walk out. Keep the power balls at the chest while your walking out

Walk out until the SB is between the scapulae, keeping the hips up.

Keep the spine neutral from hip to head. Maintain a tight core and look at the ceiling.

Allow one power ball to go behind the head, keeping the other at the chest. Perform alternating pullovers.

27) Dumbbell supine diagonal crossover
TEACHING CUES:

These supine diagonal crossovers really challenge the upper back and posterior shoulder.

Sit on the SB and put the DB on the thighs. Lean back as your feet walk out. Keep the DB at the chest while your walking out

Walk out until the SB is between the scapulae, keeping the hips up.

Take the DB and perform a diagonal pattern. Add rotation at the end of the pattern.

28) Power ball supine diagonal crossover
      TEACHING CUES:

For additional gripping demand, a Power Ball can be implemented.

Sit on the SB and put the Power Ball on the thighs. Lean back as your feet walk out. Keep the power ball at the chest while your walking out

Walk out until the SB is between the scapulae, keeping the hips up.

Take the power ball and perform a diagonal pattern. Add rotation at the end of the pattern.

Balance and Stability Exercises

Purpose:

The following exercises are designed to provide balance and stability. Some are repeats from other sections. However, the balance section would not be complete without their inclusion. Due to the Stabilization Limited Training methodology and the unstable nature of the SB, **all SB exercises are core and balance exercises**. All balance should be performed slow and under deliberate control.

1) Sitting pelvic tilts
TEACHING CUES:

> This exercise is a great way to introduce the "feel" of the Stability Ball. Many individuals who have never been on a Stability Ball have found this exercise challenging.
>
> Sit on the ball. Without moving any part of your body, roll and tilt your hips from side to side. Use your core muscle to move the hips
> . Stay up tall and keep the core tight.

2) Sitting knee lifts
TEACHING CUES:

> The sitting knee lift is harder than it looks.
> Sit up tall on the SB, keeping the core tight.
> Slowly lift one foot off the ground and balance.

3) Sitting knee lifts with extended leg
TEACHING CUES:

Once you master the knee lift try extending the leg. Extending the leg changes the center of mass and adds to the balance requirement.

Follow the cues for #2 and extend the knee of the raised leg.

4) Four point balance progression
TEACHING CUES:

The four-point balance is a fundamental intermediate balance exercise.

Shown here, is the sequence used to teach this balance.

Starting with both hands on the ground, each hand is separately placed on the ball to show control.

Mount the ball as to perform a push-up (hands on floor and thighs on the SB).

Tuck your knees in and walk back until you art sitting on your lower legs and the hands are close to the ball.

Bring one hand to the ball and put it back on the floor. The same with the other hand.

When the single hand control is mastered, try placing both hands to the ball.

Eventually, try to extend the leg to a 90-degree flexion at the knees. This is called a four point balance.

5) Two point balance (on knee)
  TEACHING CUES:

> Once the four-point balance has been mastered, one can try to get up on the knees. After a little practice, most individuals can succeed at this balance.
>
> From the bear balance, shift your weight back and extend the trunk to an up-right position.
>
> Keep the core tight and look straight ahead.
>
> Try to fully extend the hips and balance on the knees - not the shins.

6) One point balance on knee
  TEACHING CUES:

> The Single knee balance requires enormous hip and quad strength and stability.
>
> From the two point balance, on the knees, release one leg and balance on the shin of the support leg
>
> Use the heel of the free leg to help you balance the exercise until you are able to balance on one knee alone.

7) Sitting balance
TEACHING CUES:

The Sitting balance is fun and adds a different component to core strength and integrity.

Make sure that beginners at this exercise start to learn against a wall or an obstacle that will prevent a backward fall.

Sit on the ball, while leaning back slightly. This brings the center of mass back and allows one to raise the legs without falling forward.

Keep the core tight and slowly remove the weight off the feet. Eventually lift the feet and balance while sitting.

8) Supine knee lift
TEACHING CUES:

This balance exercise is extremely difficult to execute properly.

Sit on the ball and walk your feet forward while rolling on the SB.

Balance the SB between your shoulder blades and lift the hip up.

Keep the core tight and belly through the spine.

Slowly, lift one leg and extend it .

Hold on to the SB with the elbows, if you need a little stability. Eventually you will not need this assistance.

Keep the hips at shoulder level and spine in neutral position..

9) Two ball pushup
TEACHING CUES:

This exercise was also featured in the Chest section. Although the push-up is traditionally an upper body strength exercise, balance is the major component and limiting factor when performed between two unstable points.

Kneel down and put a hand on each SB. Extend the legs and balance in a push-up position.

Keeping the core tight and body straight, lower your chest between the SBs. Push back up to a lockout position.

Keep the SB together when learning. Then, separate the SB for addition balance requirements.

10) Ball and rocker board pushups
TEACHING CUES:

Rocker boards can be added to create different planes of instability.

As you can see, balance is again emphasized over strength.

Get into a four-point stance – on hands and knees. With the SB in front of you, put you feet on the rocker-board. Place the SB under your chest and extend the knees.

When you can balance in this position, pushup off the SB.

11) Medicine and stability ball explosive pushup
    TEACHING CUES:

> Medicine balls can be incorporated to add a different support component. Being harder and smaller, they change the hand placement and stability requirements of the arms and upper body.
>
> Balance as if you were going to perform a push-up (hands on floor).
>
> Place a medicine ball between the hands.
>
> Explode up on to the medicine ball with both hands.
>
> Keep the core tight and belly through the spine.

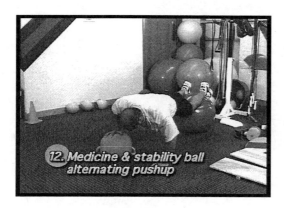

12) Medicine and stability ball alternating pushup
    TEACHING CUES:

> Core strength is essential to perform this advanced move.
>
> The placement of the stability ball may vary the difficulty as you master the exercise.
>
> Balance in a push-up position with a medicine ball under one hand.
>
> Pop up and hop over the medicine ball. Change hand positions in mid air.
>
> Learn this exercise with the SB under the knees. Eventually move the SB out to the feet.

13. Biofoam & stability ball pushup

13) Biofoam and stability ball pushup
TEACHING CUES:
The Biofoam rollers can also be used to create a different balancing stimulus. You can use different placements to change the balancing environment.

Use the cues from the push-ups (in chest section).

Get into a push-up position with the Biofoam in front of your hands.

Place one hand at a time on to the Biofoam and balance. Perform a push-up.

14. Shock lockout

14. Shock lockout

14) Shock lockouts
TEACHING CUES:
Impact training is essential to all contact sports.

Shocks are an excellent way to train an individual to absorb energy through impact without training the body in an abusive manner.

By bouncing off the ball, one learns how to make the body rigid at the moment of impact, followed by an immediate defensive response (the push).

Balance with the hands on the SB. Release the hand support and drop your body on the ball. Catch your self as you bounce back and off the ball to a "lockout" arm position.

136

15) Acyclic impact training abducted shoulder
TEACHING CUES:

A Single joint can be isolated, as shown here with the shoulder.

Kneel down and place a SB anywhere around you (shown here from the side). Place your hand on it to stabilize.

Have a partner lightly tap the SB from all angles while you try to stabilize the SB in place.

Close your eyes for additional proprioceptive demands.

16) Acyclic impact training one arm lockout
TEACHING CUES:

The entire body really achieves the benefit of this Push-up lock out position.

Balance in a push-up position (hands on SB). Go to a single arm balance.

Keep the core tight and belly through the spine.

Have a partner lightly tap the SB from all angles while you try to stabilize the SB in place.

Close your eyes for additional proprioceptive demands.

17) Acyclic impact training standing and mobility
   TEACHING CUES:

You can perform acyclic impact training standing using different stances and incorporating mobility.

If you want to really put your proprioception and kinesthetics to the test, perform standing acylcic impact training with your eyes closed.

Stand and hug the SB. Use any stance.

Keep the core tight and belly through the spine.

Have a partner lightly tap the SB from all angles while you try to stabilize the SB in place.

Add movement for additional stabilization and balance requirements.

Close your eyes for additional proprioceptive demands.

Leg and Hip Exercises

Purpose:

The following exercises are designed to provide leg and hip strength. The SB is a great tool to teach squatting for those having difficulty learning this basic move. The SB also allows one to effectively deal with balance while developing functional strength. The diversity of exercise intensity makes this modality one of the most versatile methods of strength training.

1) Back Wall Slide – 2 legs
TEACHING CUES:

Back wall slides on 2 legs is the first in the wall slide progression.

Foot positioning can accommodate lack of flexibility at the ankle, knee or hip joints.

Place the ball at the belt line and step forward about 12-14 inches in front of the ball.

Start with the feet in a shoulder width stance.

Maintain the back perpendicular to the ground with the hips underneath the shoulders and focal point to the front.

Squat down as far as good form will allow.

Keep the core tight and belly through the spine.

Keep the feet flat throughout the entire squatting motion.

As ankle flexibility and strength permits, slowly progress the feet towards the wall until they are underneath the body. At this point, bodyweight squats may be attempted.

Medicine balls and dumbbells can be used to load this exercise.

2) Back Wall Slide – 1 leg
      TEACHING CUES:

            Back wall slides on a single leg are a great way to introduce anyone to unilateral leg work. They are excellent for developing hip, knee and ankle stability.

            Use the same cues used in #1.

            Make sure the center of the foot is lined-up along the center of the body, not under the hip.

            Start with 1/4 squats and slowly increase the depth of the squatting to about 90-degree of knee flexion.

3) Back Wall Slide – 1 leg- free leg extended
      TEACHING CUES:

            One-leg, back wall slides can be made more challenging by varying the "free-leg" position. Here, the "free leg" is extended and stabilized pointing forward. This provides additional hip-flexsor and lower abdominal requirement –especially on the "free leg" side..

            Try pointing the "free-leg" in different directions. This changes the center of mass and further challenges proprioceptive demands of the supporting extremity.

4 Front wall slides-two legs

4) Front Wall Slides – 2 legs
TEACHING CUES:

Front wall slides add a different dimension to squatting work.

This exercise is very specific to forward locomotion, putting tremendous stability demands on the lower leg.

It usually takes a couple of attempts to figure out the most comfortable angle of lean.

A 60 to 70-degree lean is well tolerated by most people.

Use hand support on the wall to help you learn the balance for this exercise.

As with the back wall slides, two-leg work is the first to be mastered.

Place the ball at the belt line and step back to allow a comfortable forward lean.

Squat down naturally – bringing the hips backwards.

Hold on to the ball or use the wall for hand support while learning the balance for this exercise.

Stay on the balls of the feet, maintaining a 90-degree angle of dorsi-flexion, through the entire exercise.

Use forward thrusting movements from the arms to get a more specific sport application.

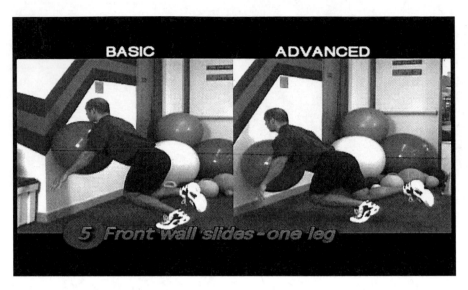

5) Front Wall Slides – 1 leg
TEACHING CUES:

Front wall slides on a single leg require an enormous amount of strength, balance and stability.

This exercise is excellent on strengthening the knee and ankle complex specific to the acceleration phase of running.

In this exercise, beginners may want to start with a higher ball position and strictly adhere to the 70-degree lean we suggested earlier. Also, a hand support on the wall may be appropriate to teach the balance component of this exercise.

As strength increases, the ball position and lean may become more aggressive to increase the intensity of this exercise.

Notice the difference between the basic and advanced versions in the beginning and finishing squat positions.

Remember to position the supporting foot in line with the center of the body, not under the hip.

Keep the heels up and the hips back as if you were accelerating off the blocks.

6) Lateral Wall Slide – 2 legs
TEACHING CUES:

Lateral wall-slides are superb for developing lateral stability in the lower body, especially, the ankle complex.

They are excellent for enhancing functional strength involved in changes of direction.

As with the other wall slides, two-leg work precedes one-leg work.

To familiarize yourself with the proper positioning, use the arm closest to the ball to stabilize yourself.

As you become more proficient at this exercise, use less of the arm support.

A 70-degree lean is a good starting point for most individuals. You can progress to 60-degree leans. Greater leans are usually not functional for most people.

Start with the ball at the belt line and feet together.

Slide down into a position resembling a skiing motion.

7) Lateral Wall Slide – 1 leg, outside leg
TEACHING CUES:

The next step is to balance on the outside leg.

This position really increases the demand for stability of the ankle complex, especially the everters of the ankle.

As with the front single leg wall slides, a higher ball position with less lean is a great starting point..

Once the basic version is mastered, the advanced form can be attempted.

Keep the knee aligned with the toes, between the hip and ankle.

Then, progress the outside foot away from the ball to increase the lean of the body to about 60 degrees.

There is no need to squat beyond a 90-100 degrees of knee flexion, since this is the angle most used in changes of direction.

Start with a 70 lean until you are comfortable with the exercise.

Use the arm closest to the wall for support while you are learning to balance for this exercise. The progress to no arm support.

144

8) **Lateral Wall Slide – 1 leg, inside leg**
   TEACHING CUES:

This is the ultimate exercise for the inverters of the ankle and intrinsic plantar musculature.

It is excellent for conditioning and prehabilitating the lower extremities of athletes.

This is an excellent exercise for kickers of any kind.

Freeze any picture of a kick just before ball contact and you will see this leg position.

This position is also very specific to the cross over step used in changes of direction to the inside.

Follow the same progression you did for the outside leg version of this exercise.

Again, this exercise has a basic and advanced version. The higher ball position facilitates a higher squat position. This reduces the intensity considerably.

Remember to use only a functional squat depth of 90-100 degrees.

This depth is sufficient to emulate knee flexion in kicking and changes of direction.

9) One-leg stability ball squat with stationary support
   TEACHING CUES:

Start the one leg series with a smaller ball and with stationary support.

This reduces the amount of hip flexor flexibility needed by the trailing leg. It also allows a lower squatting position.

The stationary support also reduces the amount of balance required to perform this exercise.

After mastering the smaller ball, one can progress to a larger ball that will increase the flexibility demands of the hip flexors of the trailing leg.

Stand on one foot and place the ball under the shin or instep of the trailing leg.

Make sure the ground-based foot is facing forward and keep the knee aligned in this direction throughout the entire exercise.

Keep the knee over the ground-based foot as you squat.

Stay tall, keep core tight and face forward.

10) One-leg squat with mobility
    TEACHING CUES:

After stationary support is mastered, mobility can then be incorporated with the smaller ball.

This mobility will greatly increase the stability requirements of the front leg and prepares an individual for "free standing, counterbalanced single leg work".

Once you feel comfortable with mobility on the smaller ball, progress to a larger ball for added flexibility demands.

Anterior reaches can be added for additional hip extensor work on the squatting side.

This exercise is one step away from free-standing one-leg, anterior, counterbalanced reaches.

Stand on a single leg and place the ball to the inside of the knee.

Place the toes of the free leg on top of the SB.

Squat, while rolling the trailing leg over the SB until it is fully extended.

Make sure the ground-based foot is facing forward and keep the knee aligned in this direction throughout the entire exercise.

Keep the knee over the ground-based foot as you squat.

Keep core tight and face forward.

11) Lateral 1-leg squat
TEACHING CUES:

Lateral squats put an enormous amount of stretch on the adductors of the ball-supported leg. They are excellent for conditioning the adductors and prehabilitating this frequently injured muscle group.

Start with smaller balls for stationary support. Then progress to larger ball for additional flexibility demands.

This is the entry level exercise to the lateral one leg squatting series.

Stand on a single leg.

Place the SB to the inside of the ground-based leg with the free leg resting on it.

Squat down, keeping the knee and foot of the ground based leg aligned.

Keep the core tight and stay as upright as possible.

Reaches can be added to add difficulty and a multi-planar stimulus to this progression.

12) Lateral 1-leg squat with mobility
TEACHING CUES:

Once the stationary support has been mastered, you can then proceed to mobility work with the ball-supported leg.

Follow all of the cues for #11.

Slide out the SB lag as you squat. This movement dynamically moves the center mass of the exercise, adding a greater demand for balance and stability.

13) Lateral 1-leg squat with mobility circles
TEACHING CUES:

> After assuming a squat position, and isometrically holding it, circles can be executed in a clockwise and counter clockwise pattern.
>
> Try figure 8s, Xs or other patterns to move the body's center of gravity and increase the balance and stability requirements.
>
> As always, keep the core tight and belly through the spine.

14) Prone 2-leg knee extension
TEACHING CUES:

> Two-leg work always comes first.
>
> Start the prone knee extensions with the ball close to the knees.
>
> Slowly move the ball support closer to the feet.
>
> This increases the moment arm of the knees, hips and abdominals.
>
> Eventually, the ball support moves to the toes.
>
> This support position really demands a high degree of stability of all the joints from the ankles to the shoulders.
>
> Balance on elbows and knees with the SB under the insteps. Keep a straight line between the shoulders and knees.
>
> Make the core tight and drive the belly in.
>
> Extend the legs without breaking the alignment of the body.

15) Prone 1-leg knee extension
TEACHING CUES:

Single-leg knee extensions on the Stability Ball greatly increases the strength and stability requirements of the core and lower extremity.

Start this exercise with the ball at the shin then proceed to the instep and toe, as shown here.

Follow the cues for #14, except on a single leg.

16) Prone 1-leg knee extension on toes
TEACHING CUES:

Your final step is to have enough ankle strength to support this toe position. Stabilizing this exercise on the toes of one leg is the ultimate in single leg stability work. All of the joints between the toes and the elbows are challenged along all planes of motion.

Follow the cues for #14 and #15.

Keep the scaplular complex stable. Maintain a posterior pelvic tilt to protect the lumbar spine.

Keep the hips extended, the knees straight and the foot pointing perpendicular to the ball.

Remember to keep perfect body alignment.

 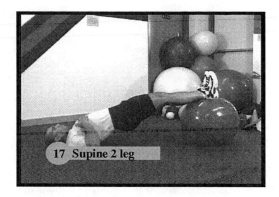

17) Supine 2-leg curls
TEACHING CUES:

Make sure you have mastered #1 from the "Hip Extensor" section before attempting this exercise.

First in the progression is always two-leg work.

In this exercise, foot position will dictate which muscles of the lower extremity you will emphasize.

A "toe up" position enhances the activation of the gastroc muscle for the lower leg.

On the other hand, pointing your toes will emphasize the hamstrings.

Lay down, facing up with the SB under the ankles.

Lift the hips into a bridge and balance. Curl the heel to the hips.

18) Supine 1-leg curl
TEACHING CUES:

One leg Supine curls are performed in the same manner as the two-leg version, however, the support requirements are doubled for the hip and knee of the supporting leg.

Follow cues for #17, except perform exercise on a single leg.

19) Supine 1-leg curl with mobility
      TEACHING CUES:

              Adding a mobility component can increase the difficulty of single-leg work.

              Here, a pattern resembling running mechanics is incorporated.

              Follow stabilization cues for #17-18.

              Mobility: While the SB leg curls, the free leg extends..

20) Large ball leg presses on 2 legs (progress with mobility to heel balance)
      TEACHING CUES:

              Two-leg work begins the progression.

              These are the easiest of the leg exercises and appropriate for any population.

              Sit on large ball and walk the feet forward while leaning back and balancing on the SB.

              Perform a squat while balancing on the SB.

              Keep body straight and core tight.

              Start with your feet flat on the ground and about shoulder width apart.

              You can add to the balance demand of the exercise by adding some mobility and reducing the support area.

              This is easily accomplished by rocking back to your heel at the end of the press. Narrowing the stance can further increase the balance demands of this exercise.

21) Large ball leg presses on 1 leg
     TEACHING CUES:

> The narrow stance of the Large Ball Leg Press progression sets you up for this single legwork.
>
> Follow cues of #20.
>
> Maintain a flat foot position on the pressing leg.
>
> The free leg may be held in an extended position.
>
> Movement to the free leg may be added for increased balance requirements.

22) Large ball leg presses on 1 leg with mobility
     TEACHING CUES:

> Once the single leg pressing is mastered.
>
> Rocking to the heel of the pressing leg reduces the support area to add difficulty to this exercise.
>
> Follow positioning and stabilization cues of #20 and #21.

23) Large ball leg presses on sidestrike
   TEACHING CUES:
>
> With a little imagination, any piece of equipment in a gym can be used with the SB.
>
> Shown here is how a Sidestrike is normally used for developing foot agility.
>
> The back angle of the Sidestrike provides a more stable leg-pressing environment at the expense of higher resistance.
>
> The trainers can always add stimuli, such as light tapping on the SB, to provide additional proprioceptive stimuli.

24) Large ball leg presses on sidestrike 1 leg
   TEACHING CUES:
>
> The single leg version is a great way to provide the lower extremity with excellent strength and stability training.
>
> The use of the Sidestrike provides a safe working environment with considerable resistance.

154

25) Large ball leg presses on 45° angled box
    TEACHING CUES:

If you don't have access to a Sidestrike, angled boxes can be used in the same manner.

However, due to the lack of rear support, this provides more stability and balance requirements while unloading the resistance.

Follow the same cues outlined for #20.

26) Large ball leg presses on 45° angled box on 1 leg
    TEACHING CUES:

After successfully completing the two-leg version of this exercise, go on to single-leg work.

This exercise gently triggers a large amount of proprioception in the lower leg.

Follow the same cues outline in #20.

27) Large ball leg presses on bench platform   1 leg
TEACHING CUES:

Here is just an example of how any surface can create a leg press environment.

Here, the thin side of a bench platform is used as a support for the feet.

This set-up can also turn into a calf-press for rehabilitation or home use.

The movement starts with two leg, heel and ball of foot support.

The progression then takes this exercise to single leg support.

Set up ball in front of a platform with beveled corners.

Sit on ball while putting your feet on the edge of the platform.

Perform a squatting motion as if you were on a hack-squat machine.

The support area of the supporting leg can be reduced to the ball of the foot.

Notice the minimal support offered by the thin bench platform.

LEGS - EXTERNAL RESISTENCE

28) **Large ball leg presses – band resisted**
    TEACHING CUES:

> Bands or pulleys can be utilized to increase the load of the Large Ball Leg presses when pressing off an angled box or any other support surface. The use of bands is encouraged over free weight implements because they provide resistance parallel to the line of force production. Follows outlined in #23-27. Wrap bands around a stable piece of equipment in such a way that the pull comes from the direction of the feet.

29) **DB back wall slides**
    TEACHING CUES:

> Adding external resistance can increase the intensity of Back Wall Slides. Although the use of dumbbells is illustrated here, medicine balls can also be utilized to add resistance to this exercise.
>
> To increase the intensity of this exercise, one can engage the upper body by supporting the external resistance at shoulder level.
>
> Follows cues outlined in #1 holding DBs in your hands.

30) DB front wall slide
TEACHING CUES:

Any weighted implement can increase the intensity of the Front wall slide. Symmetrical loading is demonstrated here.

However, asymmetrical loading can also be used to provide a higher degree of balance and neurological demand.

Remember to stay on the balls of the feet, keeping the back in a lordotic position.

Follow cues outlined in #4 while holding DBs in your hands. A shoulder or hang position can be used when holding the DBs.

31) DB lateral wall slide
TEACHING CUES:

Lateral wall slides can be made more challenging by adding resistance. A dumbbell is used for illustrative purposes.

Progress from two foot to single foot support and vary the weight position for added support demands and balance requirements.

Regardless of foot position, start with a 70-degree lean to get accustomed to this exercise, then work your way to a more aggressive lean.

Follow cues outlined in #6 while holding DB at shoulder height. Use the outside hand to support the DB.

32) DB lateral wall slide – one leg, outside leg
   TEACHING CUES:

> After the two-leg version, the outside leg can be challenged unilaterally.
>
> The external resistance can be supported at shoulder height for increased upper body isometric work.
>
> Follow cues outlined in #7 while holding DB at shoulder height. Use the outside hand to support the DB.

33) DB lateral wall slide – one leg, inside leg
   TEACHING CUES:

> The inside leg version of the lateral wall slide can be made more challenging by adding external resistance and supporting it at shoulder level.
>
> Follow cues outlined in #8 while holding DB at shoulder height. Use the outside hand to support the DB.

34) DB one leg squat with mobility
TEACHING CUES:

Mobility can be added to the trailing leg to increase the demands of the basic one leg stability ball squat

Dumbbell placement can also be adjusted to further increase the stability demands of the exercises.

The further away the dumbbells are dropped from the mainline of the body the greater the core and hip strength is required.

Follow cues outlined in #10 while holding DBs .

35) Lateral one leg squat
TEACHING CUES:

Here, a Power ball is used as the method of external resistance.

By changing the drop of the Power ball to the outside of the foot, one increases the motion in the transverse plane.

Follow cues outlined in #11 while holding DB or power ball in the "non-ground-based." Drop the weight to the inside of the ground based leg.

TOTAL BODY COMPOUNDS
EXTERNAL RESISTANCE

Compounds are an excellent way to efficiently train the entire body. They provide the best of all worlds: metabolic conditioning, strength and balance. There is an infinite number of exercises and combinations you can use to keep your training interesting. An extensive review of complex training with DB coumpounds can be found in our Essence of Dumbbell Training Vol. I.

1& 2)   Wall slides to alternating curls
TEACHING CUES:

The squat and curl is a popular free-standing compound.

The sequence of the curling motion can be varied to accent the ascent or descent of the exercise.

Squats can be combined with alternating curls to create a demanding two-movement compound.

The curling motion can be alternated to create a different version of this exercise.

Follow the cues outline the back wall slide. Add various curling patterns .

Place the DB between your feet.

Put the ball between you and wall. Place ball at belt line.

Slightly bend your knees and perform a deadlift motion to pick up the DBs.

Due to the mechanics involved in getting into position – heavy weights are not recommended for this exercise.

If spotters are available to hand DB to you – heavier training can be attempted.

3) Wall slides to press
TEACHING CUES:

Back wall slides can be performed in combination with presses.

The order of the movements can be changed to adjust the flexibility demands of the exercise.

Pressing during the ascent of the squatting motion requires less shoulder flexibility and allows the implementation of heavier loads.

Pressing during the descent of the squat increases the requirement for shoulder strength and flexibility.

Follow cues outlined in the back wall slide while pressing the DBs overhead. Use various pressing patterns.

4) Wall slide, curl and press
TEACHING CUES:

Wall Slides can be combined with curls and presses to form a three movement compound.

In this version the curling takes place on the ascent of the squat and the pressing during the descent.

Try reversing the order to create a different pattern and exercise

Follow cues outline in the back wall slide while curling and pressing the DBs overhead. Use various pressing and curling patterns.

5) Wall slide, alternating curl and press
TEACHING CUES:

Here is an example of how changing the sequence and pattern of the exercises in one compound can help create a new compound.

The curl and press is being performed in a contra-lateral fashion. This certainly increases the demand for stabilization, balance and strength.

Notice the sequence was also changed to alternating right left patterns.

Follow cues outlined in the back wall slide while curling and pressing the DBs overhead in an alternating pattern. Use various order and patterns of executions.

6) Wall slide to lateral
TEACHING CUES:

Traditional single joint exercises will take on a new dimension when sequencing them with Wall Slides.

Here, a lateral raise is performed while descending to the squat portion of a Wall Slide.

Alternating the sequence, the lateral raise is performed on the ascent of the squatting motion.

For a real stability challenge, try a contra-lateral pattern of execution.

Follow cues outlined in the back wall slide while performing a lateral. Use various order and patterns of executions.

7) Wall slide to alternating front and lateral raises
TEACHING CUES:

An alternating front and lateral raise combination is just another way to change the sequence and loading parameter of this exercise.

Follow cues outlined in the back wall slide while performing a front DB raise. Use various order and patterns of executions.

8) One leg squat to press
TEACHING CUES:

One Leg Stability Ball squats also lend themselves to compound training.

Here, an overhead press is combined with the one-leg squat.

The single leg support makes this exercise classification much more demanding than the previous Wall Slides compounds.

The use of larger balls increases the flexibility demands of the hip flexors of the trailing leg.

Follow the cues outlined in the one leg SB squat while holding the DB at the shoulders.

9) **Lateral one leg squat and snatch**
   TEACHING CUES:

One leg-work can also be combine with more explosive exercises.

Snatches with the Power ball add additional gripping requirements as well as increased emphasis on transverse motion.

The rotational mechanics of this exercise increase the load in the transverse plane and really escalates the neural demand of this exercise.

The mobility of the leg prepares the individual for the counterbalance motion, many times used in free-standing single legwork.

Follow cues outlined in the lateral one leg SB squat while holding on the DB with the non-ground-based hand.

When coming up from the squat, pull on the DB as if you were starting a lawn mower. Create enough momentum in the DB so that it travels to a lockout position overhead.

Abdominals - Obliques Exercises

Purpose:

The purpose of the following exercises is to provide strength to the ventral musculature. We will illustrate some traditional applications, as well as some more innovative approaches to training the abdominals and obliques. You will see some of the exercises in this section and in other sections, due to their multipurpose nature.

1) **Floor crunches – feet on ball**
   TEACHING CUES:

   > Crunches are the most basic abdominal exercises on the stability ball.
   > Here, the stability ball is used to elevate the feet.
   > This position is excellent for beginners to learn what a posterior pelvic tilt feels like.
   > It also serves to acquaint them with the balance of the stability ball.
   > The basic crunch makes a great combination with supine bridges and supine rotations for a basic core protocol.
   > By moving the arm position further from the hips, one creates more resistance due to the longer moment arm produced.
   > An ABC pattern can also be incorporated to introduce movement along the body's transverse plane.
   > Notice the 90 degrees of hip and knee flexion in the reference position of this exercise.
   > Lie down and secure the SB between your hips and ankles.
   > Bring the belly through the spine. We like to teach a posterior pelvic tilt from this position. It's not a functional position, however, we use it to provide an extra level of safety for many exercises.
   > Crunch up until your shoulder blades are up off the ground. Exhale while crunching.

166

2) Floor supine rotations (ball on floor → ball in air → mobility)
   TEACHING CUES:

   Supine rotations provide very mild rotation mechanics for the obliques.

   They are also excellent for providing a mild stretch for the lower back, as well. However, lifting the ball off the ground and adding mobility really escalates the intensity of this exercise.

   Lie down as you would perform a crunch.

   Keep the shoulders flat on the ground during the entire exercise.

   Roll the ball form side to side.

3) Floor reverse crunches (progress to ABCs)
   TEACHING CUES:

   Reverse crunches further emphasize the posterior pelvic tilt. This position is used for all advanced exercises where the body is supported between two distal points. Strictly from a safety perspective.

   Proper ball sizing will make this exercise easier.

   Squeeze the ball between your heels and you glutes.

   Sometimes pointing your feet will allow your heel to aid in securing the ball in place. An ABC pattern can be added to increase the rotational mechanics of this exercise.

   Lie down as you would perform a crunch.

   Keep the shoulders flat on the ground during the entire exercise.

   Pick up the ball between the hips and the heels.

4) Floor full crunches
TEACHING CUES:

A crunch and reverse crunch can be combined to provide more a pronounced trunk flexion exercise.

These full crunches can also be performed in an ABC pattern to bring in greater involvement from the Obliques.

Arm position can be adjusted away from the hips to increase the resistance of this exercise.

Lie down facing up feet on the ball. Simultaneously crunch and pick up the ball.

5) Partial abdominal crunch
TEACHING CUES:

Once a good base of core strength has been developed, one can proceed to partial crunches on top of the ball. This requires a higher degree of balance than its floor exercise equivalents.

Light spotting may be appropriate until an individual gets acquainted to this new unstable exercise environment.

This partial range of motion maintains the longest moment arm possible for this exercise. This really puts the abdominals under tension during the entire time of the exercise.

Sit on the ball and walk your feet forward until the SB is under the belt line. Crunch up to about 45-degree.

6) Full abdominal crunch
TEACHING CUES:

The additional movement of the full abdominal crunch really increases the need for balance. The increased range of motion continuously changes the center of mass, elevating the balance demands of this exercise.

Sit on the ball and walk your feet forward until the SB is under the belt line.

Crunch up to an upright posture. Keep the core tight and belly through the spine. Keep the cervical spine neutral. Exhale during the crunch.

7) Lateral crunch (hips on ball / feet on floor)
TEACHING CUES:

Lateral crunches are a traditional exercise for unilateral abdominals and lower back development. They can be performed on a stability ball to add stabilization demands.

This is one of those rare times where stabilizing the feet will enhance the exercise. You can use any support base or a partner to aid in stabilizing your feet.

This exercise will be easier to perform if the top leg trails back.

Sit on the ball and walk your feet forward until the SB is under the belt line. Roll on your side and secure the feet against a wall or under a bench. Crunch up to about 45-degrees.

8) **Diagonal crunch (progress to lifting leg to opposite elbow)**
   TEACHING CUES:

> Diagonal crunches are extremely difficult to balance.
> This is by far the limiting aspect of this exercise.
> A proper firing sequence of the core musculature is essential for proper balance.
> Use a hand and arm support on the SB to help you balance the exercise.
> Follow cues outline for #7. Crunch the elbow to the opposite knee.

9) **Acyclic impact training push-up lock out (2arm   1arm)**
   TEACHING CUES:

> The entire body really gets the benefit of this Push-up lock out position.
> However, what keeps it all together is the core!
> Get into a "hands on ball" push-up position.
> Have a partner tap the SB in a random manner. Try to stabilize the SB under you.
> Go to a single arm stabilization for increased difficulty.

170

10) Acyclic impact training standing and mobility
TEACHING CUES:

You can perform acyclic impact training standing using different stances or incorporating mobility.

If you want to really put your proprioception and kinesthetics to the test, perform standing acylcic impact training with your eyes closed.

Stand and hug the SB. Use various foot positions (e.g. parallel, staggered, etc.) and add movement to increase the demands of this exercise.

11) Acyclic impact training shock lockouts
TEACHING CUES:

Shock lockouts are an excellent way to prepare the core to absorb impact without training it in an abusive manner.

This exercise simulates the chaotic nature of impact absorption in sports.

Get into a "hands on ball" push-up position.

Drop your body onto the ball. As you bounce back off the ball, lockout to a stabilized position.

ABDOMINALS/OBLIQUES
EXTERNAL RESISTANCE

12) Sitting diagonal swing
TEACHING CUES:

> The following swings were also featured in our shoulder section of Vol 1. However, they are so impressive in developing core stability we could not leave them out of this core section.
>
> The core is the primary stabilizer of this exercise while also providing excellent work for the accelerators and decelerators of the arm.
>
> The use of a Converta Ball is preferred for this exercise. However, Power balls or other implements could also be utilized.
>
> Sit on the SB. Hold on to the rope of the Converta ball using a golfer's grip.
>
> Swing the ball in a diagonal pattern. Keep the core tight.

13) Sitting side swings
TEACHING CUES:

> Side swings further focuses on the transverse plane. This plane of movement mainly is governed by the core of the body, especially when sitting on the Stability ball.
>
> Follow cues for #12. Swing the ball in a horizontal direction.

14. Giant overhead swing

14) Giant overhead swing
TEACHING CUES:

These swings not only address shoulder overhead mechanics.

They are supported and made possible by the stability of the trunk.

The rope attachment of the Converta ball allows one to control the moment arm and resistance of this exercise.

Follow cues for #12. Swing the ball in a horizontal direction.

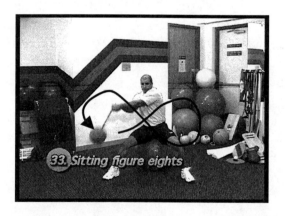

33. Sitting figure eights

15) Sitting figure 8s
TEACHING CUES:

Figure 8s also provide enormous core work.

Again the use of the Coverta-Ball is recommended due to the rope attachment.

The additional length of the rope significantly increases the demand on core, shoulders and wrists – especially in the sitting position.

Sit on the SB. Hold on to the rope of the Converta ball using a golfer's grip.

Swing the ball in a figure 8 pattern. Keep the core tight.

16) Rotations (supine)
   TEACHING CUES:

Rotations can be performed with a variety of weighted implements.

Illustrated here is the use of a dumbbell and rubber tubing.

However, medicine balls are also an excellent choice.

Keep the hip at about shoulder level and maintain a wide foot support base to help you stabilize this movement.

Sit on the SB while holding on to the band.

Walk your feet forward and slide over the SB until your belt line is on top of the SB.

Lockout your arms and hold the band in front of your chest.

Roll the SB from side to side as you rotate the upper body.

Keep the hips high and core tight.

17) Rotations, 1 arm (supine)
   TEACHING CUES:

These one arm rotation address forehand and backhand mechanics.

The power-ball really increases the gripping demands making this exercise ideal for racket sport athletes. The lower body rotation also addresses rotational mechanics at the hip and knee.

Sit on the SB while holding on the band.

Walk your feet forward and slide over the SB until your belt line is on top of the SB.

Lockout your arms and hold the Power ball in front of your chest.

Roll the SB from side to side as you rotate the upper body. Keep the hips high and core tight.

174

18) DB crunches (straight and diagonal)
   TEACHING CUES:

Resisted crunches will increase the stabilization and strength requirement of the standard crunch.

Diagonal patterns can be incorporated to increase the strength demands along the body's transverse plane.

Once again, a dumbbell is being used to demonstrate this exercise.

Sit on the ball and hold on the weight using DB, Power ball or medicine ball.

Hold the weight at your chest.

Walk your feet forward until the SB is under the lumbar spine.

Crunch up to about 45-degrees.

Hip Extensor - Lumbar Exercises

Purpose:

The exercises in this section target the extensor mechanism. The supine exercises provide a wide spectrum of application. All populations tolerate most of them and the single leg versions challenge our elite athletes. The prone progressions range from mild resistance to explosive applications.

1) **Two-leg bridges**
   TEACHING CUES:

> Two legged bridges are the most basic lumbar and hip extensor exercise that can be done on the stability ball.
>
> It is part of our standard protocol; Crunch, Bridge and Rotations (CBRs).
>
> Consistent with the lever system inherent to stability ball training, the closer the ball is to the feet the longer lever arm and the harder the exercise becomes.
>
> The arm position can start wide (i.e. arms opened facing the floor) and eventually narrow the support (i.e. hands on chest, elbows on the ground).
>
> Lay down putting your lower leg on the SB.
>
> Slowly lift your hips as high as possible. Bring the hips down and stop short of reaching the floor.

2) One-leg bridge
TEACHING CUES:

The basic bridge can be converted to an advanced exercise by performing it with a single leg support.

Lay down putting a single leg on the SB. Keep the other in the air.

Slowly lift your hips as high as possible. Bring the hips down and stop short of reaching the floor.

This exercise can be started with ball support under the calf and eventually taken to the heel.

Once this version of this exercise is mastered, mobility to the free leg can be added to increase the stability and strength demands of this exercise.

3) Hip lifts supported on ball of feet
TEACHING CUES:

Hip lifts are similar to bridges; therefore, follow the cues for #1.

However, the lower body is supported on the SB, by the ball of the foot instead of higher on the leg.

The "ball of the foot supports and creates a longer moment arm increasing the torque at the hips.

Hip lifts are excellent for strengthening the extensor chain at the specific angle of the foot plant during running.

4) Hip lifts supported on ball of one foot
 TEACHING CUES:

Single leg Hip lifts become increasingly specific to running.

Since most pulled hamstrings in running occur during the plant phase, this exercise is a great prehabilitator for all sprinting athletes.

Single leg support also brings in a stability component along the transverse plane of the body.

Follow cues outlined in #2, except the only part of the lower leg touching the SB should be the ball of the foot.

Triple Threat (TT)Progression:

1) All exercises in the TT should be individually mastered and part of the current training program.

2) Prior to attempting the TT, the trainee should be able to complete 3 sets of 10 reps of each of the exercises within an hour training session.

3) Start with two-leg version. 3 sets of 5 reps of each of the TT exercises (i.e. 15 total reps). 1-2 times per week. Add 2 reps of each of the exercises per week.

4) At week number 5, you should be at 3 sets of 15 reps – on two legs.

5) Week six –go to a single leg and drop back down to 5 reps per exercise (i.e. 15 total reps). Add 2 reps to each TT exercise every week.

6) At week 10, you should be at a set of :

15 single leg bridges
15 single leg curls
15 single leg hip lifts
Consequtively – 45 reps!
Without putting you hips down!
Now you have "hamstrings of steel"

5) **Triple threat combo**
   TEACHING CUES:

The SB progression to develop **hamstrings of steel** is the **Triple Threat**.

This combination exercise incorporates the **supine bridge, supine leg curls and the hip tilts** sequenced without rest.

Most fit individuals work up to 3 sets of 15 reps of each exercise on two legs. Our athletes go on to single leg work

6) **Triple threat combo with one leg**
   TEACHING CUES:

After the two-leg version of the Triple Threat is mastered, one leg-work is the next step – see progression above.

Elite athletes can eventually turn in 3 sets of 15 reps of each exercise – That's 45 successive reps without resting!

Notice that once the hips come up off the floor, they stay up for the duration of the exercise.

7) Ball supported contra-lateral supermans
TEACHING CUES:

Contra-lateral supermans are one of the most basic lumbar and hip exercises that can be done on the stability ball.

However, they engage the entire extensor chain and really recruit some muscle.

Assume a four-point stance and place the ball under your trunk.

Extend one arm out by flexing the shoulder. At the same time extend the opposite leg. Perform exercise slow and under control.

Keep entire spine straight and keep the core tight.

8) Kneeling prone hypers
TEACHING CUES:

These prone hypers on the knees target the muscles of the lower back.

They are a great way to focus on the lumbar spine without engaging the hips and hamstrings.

Assume a four-point stance and place the ball under your trunk.

Extend the spine and lift your upper body as upright as it will go.

Arm placement can range from laced behind the head (no pressure on the neck) to extend out.

Keep the cervical spine straight –regardless of hand position.

Extending the arms is a great way to increase the moment arm of this exercise. This not only adds more resistance to the lumbar musculature, it's also excellent for the external rotators of the arms and postural muscles of the upper back.

9) 3 point prone hypers (supported on balls of feet)
      TEACHING CUES:

These prone hypers also focus on the lumbar spine.

However, the extended hip position increases the stabilization demands of the glutes and hamstrings.

Assume a three-point stance (SB and feet) and place the ball under your naval.

Extend the spine and lift your upper body as upright as it will go.

Arm placement can range from laced behind the head (no pressure on the neck) to extend out.

Keep the cervical spine straight – regardless of hand position.

As with the previous prone hypers, arms movement can increase the intensity of the exercise.

10) Reverse hypers
      TEACHING CUES:

Reverse hypers are excellent for developing great hip extension.

Place SB under the hips and secure the elbows on the ground.

Always maintain a neutral cervical spine. Rest your head on your hands.

Slowly lift your legs while maintaining them straight. Lift them until the body is straight.

Do not allow the shoulders to rock back and forth, or up and down.

11) One leg reverse hypers with contra-lateral, knee balance
TEACHING CUES:

The intensity of Reverse hypers can be increased by progressing to contra-lateral work.

Single knee support with contra-lateral hip extension requires exception rotational stability along the body's transverse plane.

Mount the ball as if you were going to perform a "hands on floor" push-up. The top of the SB should be at about the thigh

Balance on one leg and perform a knee tuck. The SB should now be under the knee with the hip and knee flexed at about 90-degrees.

Raise the free leg while maintaining a single leg knee tuck balance.

12) One leg hypers with contra-lateral hip flexion, toe balance
TEACHING CUES:

The ultimate in contra-lateral hip work is illustrated here.

The toe balance on the flexed leg engages all of the joints from the toes to the supporting hands.

The extending hip is truly challenged due to the flexed position of the contra-lateral hip.

Mount the ball as if you were going to perform a "hands on floor" push-up. The top of the SB should be a bit below the knee.

Balance on one leg and perform a knee tuck. The SB should now be under the toes with the hip and knee flexed at about 90-degrees.

Raise the free leg while maintaining a single leg knee tuck balance.

13) Explosive hypers
TEACHING CUES:

Once the proper strength base has been developed with the hypers and reverse hypers, explosive work can be performed.

The whole idea here is to elevate your body off the ball.

This requires a tight core, perfect timing, killer abdominal deceleration capabilities and explosive power.

Assume a four-point stance (feet and hands) and place the ball under your belt line.

Explosively extend the spine, lifting your arm and feet at the same time.

Reset your position after each rep.

Don't get discouraged –it takes a while to get this one right.

Hip Flexor - Abdominal Exercises

Purpose:

The exercises in this section will provide excellent training for the flexor chain. Although the supine position is really not very functional for most people, the training with the SB provides and adds a new dimension to stabilization and core strength. We have seen this exercises really enhance functional movements, such as running and jumping. Some of these exercises will be old favorites (even if outdated) - others will be new. The objective is to give the reader as much of the "new and old" to make this form of training user friendly and acceptable to all.

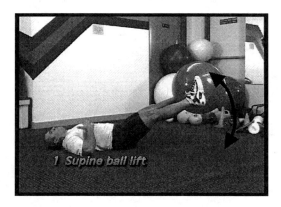

1 Supine ball lift

1) Supine ball lift
TEACHING CUES:

This good, old fashion leg lift is made a bit more interesting by grabbing a stability ball between the feet.

People with lower-back conditions should not attempt this exercise.

A prerequisite to this exercise is passing the abdominal test discussed in the "teaching cues and recommendations" section.

Lay down keeping the lumber spine flat on the ground and the belly drawn in.

Place the SB between your feet and lift it slowly to about 30-40 degrees.

2) Lateral lying ball lift
TEACHING CUES:

Side lying Ball lifts work the core in a unilateral fashion while providing good hip abductor and adductor conditioning.

Lay down on your side, keeping the trunk flat on the ground and the core tight.

Place the SB between your feet and lift it slowly to about 30-40 degrees.

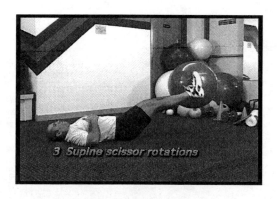 

3) Supine leg scissor rotations
TEACHING CUES:

Supine leg scissors are great for transition work in between heavy strength training, like bench pressing.

Getting the proper foot position and balance for the ball rotation requires some work.

Lay down keeping the lumber spine flat on the ground and the belly drawn in.

Place the SB between your feet and lift it slowly to about 30-40 degrees.

Rotate the ball with your feet.

Keep the lower back flat on the ground during the entire exercise.

This ensures protection of the lumbar spine.

185

4) Lateral leg scissor rotations
TEACHING CUES:

Supine leg scissors are the most basic exercise of this series.

Getting the proper foot position and balance for the ball rotation requires some work.

Lay down on your side, keeping the trunk flat on the ground and the core tight.

Place the SB between your feet and lift it slowly to about 30-40 degrees.

Rotate the ball with your feet.

Keep the trunk flat on the ground during the entire exercise.

Keep core tight during the entire exercise.

5) Flexed knee ball exchanges twisting
TEACHING CUES:

Performing this ball exchange with flexed knees results in a shorter moment arm in this exercise.

An alternating pattern can be added to ball exchanges to provide some motion along the body's transverse plane.

Lay down keeping the lumber spine flat on the ground and the belly drawn in.

Hold the SB with your hands.

Tuck your knees towards the chest and place the SB between your feet.

Straighten out the body. Tuck again and grab the SB with your hands.

Repeat cycle.

186

6) Straight leg ball exchanges
TEACHING CUES:

Ball exchanges really test abdominal and hip strength as well as coordination.

Notice that the scapular complex is lifted off the floor during the pike portion of this exercise.

This requires the proper sequence of core muscle contraction.

The ball, arms and legs are maintained off the floor during the entire time of this exercise.

Lay down keeping the lumber spine flat on the ground and the belly drawn in.

Hold the SB with your stretched out hands.

Flex your hips while lifting your upper body and raising your straight legs.

Place the SB between your feet.

Straighten out the body. Tuck again and grab the SB with your hands.

Repeat cycle.

7) Prone knee tucks – 2 legs
TEACHING CUES:

Two leg knee tucks are the first in the progression.

They not only focus on core development but also require good upper-body stabilization.

They are an excellent way to introduce a beginner to prone stability ball work.

Mount the SB as if you were going to perform a "hands on floor" push-up. Walk out till the top of the SB is under the knees.

Tuck the knees to the chest. Straighten out and repeat.

Keep the core tight, especially when you straighten out.

8) Prone knee tucks – 1 leg
TEACHING CUES:

These one leg knee tucks increase the demands for rotational stabilization and balance.

Mount the SB as if you were going to perform a "hands on floor" push-up. Walk out till the top of the SB is under the knees.

Balance on one leg and keep the other lifted in the air.

Tuck the knee of the SB leg to the chest. Straighten out and repeat.

Keep the core tight, especially when you straighten out.

Keep the core tight with a posterior pelvic tilt while keeping the hips horizontally stable.

To walk out to a single leg position, begin by walking out using two-leg ball support.   Then progress to a single leg walkout.

9) Prone knee tucks – 1 leg – toe
TEACHING CUES:

These one leg tucks are the most advanced of this series.

Follow the cues outlined in #8 except go to the toes instead of the knee.

The single toe support not only challenges the core and hips, it also engages the ankle complex dorsi flexion mechanism.

10) Prone log rolls
TEACHING CUES:

Log rolls introduce dynamic rotational mechanics into the prone position. This exercise not only develops core strength and balance, it also addresses upper body coordinated support mechanics along the transverse plane.

Mount the SB and walk out till the SB is under the thighs or knees.

Keeping your body straight, rotate the hips while rolling the SB side to side.

Maintain good scapular stability and keep the hips straight. Do not allow the hips to fall below shoulder level.

A posterior pelvic tilt will ensure proper lumbar spine integrity for beginners.

11) Prone J strokes
TEACHING CUES:

J strokes combine log rolls and knee tucks and will get you ready for the skier progression that follows.

Although only the two-leg version is shown here, a single leg version of the J stroke can also be included in the progression.

Mount the SB and walk it out till the knees are on top of the SB.

Perform a knee tuck while rotating (e.g. log roll).

Come back to the starting position and repeat to the other side.

12) Prone skiers on 2 legs
TEACHING CUES:

Prone skiers continue the emphasis on core rotation.

The ball support on the knees not only requires hip stability, it creates a longer moment arm from the hip. This dramatically increases the demand for core strength along the body's transverse plane, especially during the eccentric phase of this exercise.

Mount the SB as if you were going to perform a "hands on floor" push-up. Walk out till the top of the SB is under the knees.

Tuck the knees until the hips and knees are flexed to 90 degrees.

Rotate the lower body and roll the SB until the side of the thighs touches the SB.

Rotate back to the prone, tucked position and rotate to opposite side.

190

13) Prone skiers on 1 leg
TEACHING CUES:

One-leg skiers really put an enormous amount of pressure on the adductor group.

Do not try this exercise unless you have mastered the previous two-leg version.

Mount the SB as if you were going to perform a "hands on floor" push-up. Walk out till the top of the SB is under the knees.

Balance on one knee and lift the free leg off the SB.

Tuck the knee of the SB leg until the hip and knee are flexed to 90 degrees.

Rotate the lower body and roll the SB until the side of the thigh touches the SB.

Rotate back to the prone, tucked position and rotate to opposite side until the inside of the thigh touches the SB.

14) Hip twisters
TEACHING CUES:

Hip twisters resemble a log roll with a scissor kick.

Due to the speed involved, rotational core stability is really challenged during this exercise.

Perform a ballistic log roll scissoring the lags at the end of the movement.

15) Prone upper body rocking
TEACHING CUES:

Prone body rocking is extremely deceiving.

Use a wide foot placement to provide an adequate support base for the lower body.

Hug the ball tight and try to rock from forearm to forearm while keeping the arms tight against the ball.

Start with a small ball, which require less strength and stability, then progress to larger balls for additional core strength and stabilization requirements.

16) Prone pike – 2 legs
TEACHING CUES:

Prone pikes are next in the prone tuck progression and will prepare any individual for the aggressive shoulder work possible on the SB.

They are essential in preparing an individual for the Pike presses

We begin the progression with the two-leg version of the prone pike. .

The closer the ball is to the hands, the more strength and flexibility are needed to assume the pike position.

Mount the SB and walk out until the SB is under the knees.

Flex the hips and tuck into a Pike position. Straighten out and repeat.

17) Prone pike – 1 leg to toe
   TEACHING CUES:

   Proceed to single leg prone pikes as shown here.

   Mount the SB and walk out until the SB is under the knees.

   Balance on one knee and lift the free leg into the air – parallel to the SB leg.

   Flex the hip of the SB lag and tuck into a Pike position where the ball of the foot is supporting the lower body on the SB.

   Straighten out and repeat.

Hip roll-outs

The hip roll-out series really tests the integrity of the complete flexor chain. The simplest hip rollout exercise is a challenge to most individuals. This progression eventually challenges flexor chain integrity from "toe nails to fingernails".

The most distinguishing characteristic of the hip rollout is the straight line from the hands to the hips. The only axis of rotation is the hip joint.

The shoulder roll out looks similar to the hip roll out. However, in the shoulder roll-out, the straight line is from the shoulders to the knees - the axis of rotation is the shoulder joint.

It is imperative that an individual be able to pass the abdominal strength test discussed at the beginning of this video. Lack of abdominal strength will risk lumbar hyper-extension.

Maintain tight abdominals with a posterior pelvic tilt at all times during roll-outs.

 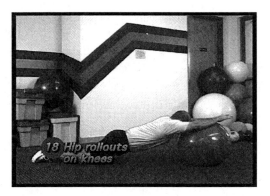

18) Hip roll-outs on knees
TEACHING CUES:

The knee support is the easiest of the hip roll-outs. This is due to the short moment arm created by the knee support. The closer the ball starts to the knees the easier the exercises will be. The idea is to start with the ball as far from the knees as possible.

Kneel in front of the SB.

Sit on your lower legs, and bend over at the hips while placing your hands on top of the SB. Your trunk and arms should be parallel with the ground.

Take your time before progressing to the next step in this progression.

194

 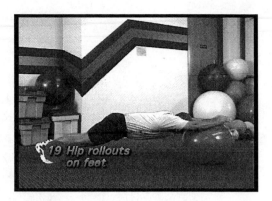

19) Hip roll-outs on feet
TEACHING CUES:

A hip roll-out, supported on the feet, is the most demanding hip flexor chain exercise on the stability ball.

The longer moment arm created by the foot support really takes the core requirement of this exercise to the elite level.

Remember to maintain proper core and shoulder mechanics during this exercise.

A strong posterior pelvic tilt and stable scapular complex are a must on this exercise.

Assume a Pike position with the feet on the ground and the hands on top of the SB.

Keeping the arms locked out, roll the hands over the SB until the body is straight.

Flex your hips again until you are back in the Pike position.

EXTERNALLY RESISTED HIP ROLLOUTS

20) Resisted hip roll-outs on knees
   TEACHING CUES:

> The only thing harder than a hip roll-out is a resisted hip roll out.
>
> Here a band is used for added resistance, however, pulleys can also be used.
>
> This is an advanced exercise and not recommended unless you have successfully completed the entire roll-out progression.
>
> Follow cues outlined in #18, while holding on to bands.
>
> Keep core tight.
>
> Hold a posterior pelvic tilt when learning this exercise.

21) Resisted hip roll-outs on feet
   TEACHING CUES:

> Roll-outs from the feet and resisted with a band, represent the most advanced hip and abdominal training the Stability ball can offer.
>
> It is elite level training and not recommended for most individuals.
>
> Follow cues outlined in #19, while holding on to bands.
>
> Keep core tight.
>
> Hold a posterior pelvic tilt when learning this exercise.

The articles within this section were written with education in mind. The conditioning professional can used them to educate clients on the use of Stability Balls and the importance of core training.

The Essence of Stability Ball Training
By
Juan Carlos Santana

One of the most versatile pieces of equipment used today by conditioning professionals is the Stability Ball (SB) (i.e. "Swiss balls", "Fit-balls", Physioballs", etc.). The SB has had long-standing success in the world of clinical rehabilitation. However, due to their effectiveness in developing balance and core strength, athletic trainers, coaches, personal trainers and physical education teachers have begun to integrate them into their programs. Now, they are the new craze in the world of athletic and functional conditioning. This article will familiarize you with the history and current applications of the SB. It will also provide some sample exercises to illustrate its versatility.

The history of the SB originates back to the early 1960s. It was made by an Italian toy maker, Aquilino Cosani, and sold primarily in Europe as the Gymnastik. In 1981, Cosani started a new company, Gymnic. These two companies are still in Italy and are the major suppliers of SBs throughout the world.

The SB's clinical application can be traced back to the 1960s, and its use by Dr. Susan Klein-Vogelbach, a Swiss PT. Through a series of classes, seminars and clinical workshops, the SB made its way to the San Francisco area in the 1980s. Since the 1980's, the SB has slowly gone from the rehabilitation setting into the fitness and athletic arena. Due to their success and growing popularity, the last decade has seen the birth of various programs developed to educate professionals on the use of SB.

The adaptability of the SB is unparalleled by any other training equipment. It allows any population to use them safely and effectively. In the home, the SB can be used to improve sitting postural mechanics while working at a desk. Adults also enjoy exercising on them due to their stimulating but gentle characteristic. Watching TV while sitting on a SB is no longer a sedentary activity. When sitting on one of these balls, one can't help but to lightly bounce and roll on them, this has been termed "active sitting".

Children of all ages can have fun with them while deriving the many benefits of exercise. The SB has been successfully used with children affected by various neurological disorders to develop balance and spatial awareness. In Europe, SBs are used in schools as chairs. Its benefits have been; improved focus, concentration, handwriting skills, better understanding of class material, and better organizational skills. There are several pilot studies in the US using SB in school. The preliminary data is comparable with that found in Europe.

Athletes use the SB to increase the neurological demand of any exercise by creating an unstable training environment. Training in this unstable training environment increases the demand for stabilization. It strengthens all of the intrinsic muscles of the core and joints. The SB is currently used by just about every major sport organization. As an example of this, Paul Callaway, PT, was the first to travel with the Professional Golf Association using the SB and resistance tubing to improve golfing performance.

The SB can be used in several ways. It can be used to support the body in various positions while performing exercise. This support can make the exercises easier or more challenging. The lever system unique to SB training, and number of limbs used for support, allows the intensity of the exercise to be controlled. Single limb support (e.g. one leg) requires more balance, thus making the exercise more difficult. Likewise, on exercises that require two distal points of support, like the push-up, the further the distance between the ball and the opposite supporting point (e.g. the arms), the harder the exercise becomes. Think of it like a bridge. The longer the bridge-span, the greater the stress on the structure and its supports.

The main characteristic of SB training is its ability to develop the core and stabilizers of the body, while addressing total body conditioning. For example, the limiting factor in performing exercises like push-ups (i.e. feet on the ball hands on the ground) is lack of core stability. Once the core has been developed to support

FIG 1

and balance the feet on the ball while performing a push-up, the progression switches support placement. That is, the hands are now supported on the ball and the feet on the ground. Since our core has been strengthen in our previous progression, the new support positions focus on the stabilizers of the upper extremities, especially the shoulder complex. I have

FIG 2

termed this type of training Stabilization Limited Training. SLT can be defined as, "training where the limiting factor in force production is not the strength of the prime movers, but rather the stabilizers that support the production of force".

During basic training, the SB can be used to support the body's weight, to keep the body aligned during exercises, or reduce the load (i.e. intensity) of an exercise.

This is illustrated in **Figures 1 and 2** with the "hyper-extension" and "crunches", respectively. In these exercises, the spine is extended or flexed while the SB supports the torso. Another basic application is using the SB to reduce the amount of weight you use in an exercise. **Figure 3**, shows how the SB can support some of the body's weight during a push-up. The different ball placements can vary the resistance to the arms and chest in accordance

FIG 3

with the strength of the individual; the further the ball is from the hands the greater the requirements for stability and strength. **Figure 4** shows a basic back "one-leg bridge" exercise that uses the SB to elevate the lower body to create resistance at the lumbar area. As with the push-up, the closer the ball is to the feet the harder the

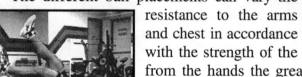

FIG 4

"bridge" becomes. In the basic application, exercise intensity can range from light rehabilitation to moderate conditioning exercises.

For more advanced training, the SB can be used to support the body in extreme positions and/or create an unstable training environment during aggressive resistance training. **Figure 5** shows this use during a "dumbbell bench press" and **Figure 6** shows how an overhead DB press can be challenged by the SB's

FIG 5

instability. The unstable nature of the SB support requires more stabilization by the shoulder joint and core for both of these exercises. **Figure 7** shows how a resisted, rotational component can be added to the "Lateral SB one leg Squat". Supporting the trailing leg on the unbalanced environment of the SB increases the balance requirement of the front leg. In **Figure 8** we see what can be done with a little imagination and a lot of functional balance and strength.

FIG 6

FIG 7

These are just some of the 300 exercises I have compiled in my two video series on Stability Ball Training. Your imagination is the only limitation to the program and exercise design on the SB. Selecting a properly sized ball is simple. The ball that will offer the most amount of versatility allows you to sit on it with you knees and hips at 90 degrees. However, using different size balls allows you more flexibility and variation with your SB training. Inflating your SBs to different pressures provides even more flexibility and complexity to the exercise environment. The higher the pressure the SB is inflated to, the more stability. Under-inflated SBs provide less stability.

For professionals, or advanced exercisers interested in learning more about SB training, there are several ways to learn about this great training modality. I have produced a two-volume video set, "The Essence of Stability Ball Training". Volume I provides 58 minutes and over 125 exercises covering the upper body and Volume II delivers 62 minutes and over 130 exercises for the lower body and core. Both volumes can be purchased by visiting our web sight **www.opsfit.com,** or by calling MF Athletic/Perform Better at 1-800-556-7464.

FIG 8

"CORE training":
Training from the inside out!
PART I
By
Juan Carlos Santana, MEd., CSCS

This article will be the first of a three part series on the development of the body's core (i.e. abdominals and lower back) for total power development. The Part I will deal with the basic premise of core development. It will offer a very basic exercise program that any healthy person will be able to perform without any difficulties. Part II will continue the discussion on the efficacy of core training and offer an intermediate program, which should be tolerated by most after the base training of the beginning program has been completed. Finally, Part III will provide a more advanced training program that will "convert" or "transfer" the strength you have developed with the previous programs to "functional power".

Power is, by far, the most predominant expression of human movement. In sports, as well as in the non-athletic arena, everything we do can be expressed as a power output. All of the things we do to make ourselves perform and feel better, whether it is to drop weight or start an exercise program, are done to inevitably improve our ability to do more work in a given time. You may think you have no need for power because you never participate in any power-oriented event. Well, if you've ever picked-up and played with a child, participated in any sport or brisk activity, or have ever reacted quickly to a slip and saved yourself from falling, you have participated in a power dominated event. Of course, if you want to improve your game in golf, tennis, basketball, football, baseball or any sport, increasing your capacity to generate power will take your play to the next level.

Most people think the "core" of the body means the abdominals. You know the muscles that all Calvin Klein models sport when posing for those fabulous billboard shots? They also think that they properly develop them by doing sit-ups or crunches. Perhaps this manner of thinking is the result of many years of an old prescription, "sit-ups and crunches for the old washboard". Few entertain the idea that the lower back plays an equally important role in stabilizing, rotating and extending the trunk. Even fewer realize the importance of the other major muscles of the core in connecting the shoulders and the hips during multi-dimensional and multi-planar movement. In fact, the main function of the body's core is not merely to flex and extend the trunk along a single plane, but to rotate and stabilize along multiple planes of motion. It is this multi-planar, rotational capacity that is behind all powerfully executed moves we praise in sports. Sampras' 130 mph serve, Tiger's 300+ drives or a house-wife moving a basket of clothing from the floor to a shelf over the right shoulder, all have the same thing in common. These moves are made possible by the power derived from the torque (rotational force) generated at various joints, especially between the hips and shoulders.

Now, lets take a look at how to approach your core conditioning. The most important consideration for safe and effective exercise is "proper PROGRESSION"- Don't run before you walk! Check with your primary care provider to make sure you do not have any contra-indications to the exercises you are about to partake in. If you have any questions as to what you are doing, consult a professional who is properly certified in the fitness field. I may start some of my sedentary or rehabilitating clients lying down, gradually move them to the kneeling position and then the standing position. The tempo of execution is also important to maximize your training. The tempo starts very slow and then, over weeks of training, progresses to a more dynamic nature. The final goal is to end up as explosive as the target activity is performed in real life(e.g. golf swing). I have three favorite pieces of equipment that I use on an everyday basis with most of my clients. These are the Stability Ball (24" or 55cm), various medicine balls (1-3kg), and rubber bands (light, medium and heavy).

One of my beginner programs with the Stability Ball consists of a Rotating Crunch (Fig 1), Hip Bridges (Fig 2) and Rotations (fig 3). Start with 1 set of 10-15 repetitions per exercise and progress to 3-4 sets of 15 repetitions per exercise. Take three-four weeks to progress from 1-4 sets, if you have not been very active. You may perform this routine 3-5 days per week.

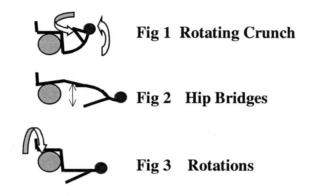

Fig 1 Rotating Crunch

Fig 2   Hip Bridges

Fig 3   Rotations

This routine will give you the foundation to handle a more challenging program. These exercises alone have helped many of my clients eliminate their chronic backaches. See you in four weeks – work hard but work smart.

"CORE training":
Training from the inside out!
PART II
By
Juan Carlos Santana, MEd., CSCS

Part II, of this three part series on core development, takes us into a more indepth discussion on the efficacy of core development. It also provides an intermediate program that is sure to take your core strength base to a new level. In turn, this new strength level will pave the way for the next step, that will be the "power conversion phase discussed in Part III.

Now, if you asked any person what training is foundational to functional power development you'll get a wide array of answers. Some will say that strength in the upper body training is the most important for power development. These individuals are easy to spot in a gym because they are the ones occupying the benches or bench press machines for hours at a time. Others will tell you that training the legs will guaranty you will get powerful. These characters are the ones who load up the leg press with all of the gym's 45-pound plates and no one is allowed to work out until their leg-work is finished. Or, they're the ones who like to permanently bend the gym' bars, and wear mouth pieces and Viking hats while squatting half-a-ton of steel. Last but not least, there is still another group who is still trying to develop power doing arm curls. The perennial, leg hiding long pants and standard tank top with 22-inch pipes easily gives them away.

My question is, who's minding the store? Who's minding the center that connects all of these important parts? Who is training the core of the body, the area between the chest and the hips? The follow-up question is, how is it being trained?

In all of the above-mentioned moves, as with all other powerful human movements, the power comes from the ground then, the legs transfer the energy to the hips. The hips then rotate and create torque between the hips and shoulders. At this point the muscles of the core come into play, contracting to bring the shoulders around to face the same direction as the hips. The extremity(s) usually serve only as an extension of the core and finally an implement (e.g. racket, club or ball.) is accelerated in the direction the hips are facing. The sequence of events I have just described is called the "kinetic chain". It stands to reason that if there is a weak link in the kinetic chain, there will be a breakdown in technique and timing, dissipation of energy and, thus, a reduction in power. In my many years of working with various populations, it is the core that is usually the weak link in the chain. Most of the time it is not due to a particular pathology, rather to a lack of proper conditioning and mechanics.

One of my favorite intermediate routines for functional core conditioning involves the use of StrechCordz bands which moves the individual to a standing position. This routine consists of a Diagonal Woodchop (Fig 1), a Reverse Diagonal Woodchop (Fig 2) and a Side Chop (Fig 3). These exercises can be performed 3-5 times per week for 3 sets of 8-12 hard reps. Stick with this program for 3-4 weeks. As a warm-up to this routine, use 1 set of 10-15 repetitions of the Stability Ball routine.

203

This routine will begin working on your balance as well as your functional strength. The resistance of the band really challenges your balance and the integrity of your base of support (i.e. your stance). My favorite stimulus of this group of exercise is their ability to strengthen while teaching the individual proper rotational mechanics. Incorrect rotational mechanics is one of the main sources of power dissipation in sports.

Start the exercises by standing with the hip facing 90^0 to the line of pull-shoulders facing the anchored end of the chord. Hold the bands, with stiffened arms always, in front of your chest. The rotation for these exercises should be initiated with the hips and then the trailing ankle, turning the ankle out. This turning out of the ankle will "release" the hips in the final direction of the turn. This is called "loading" or "opening up" the hips. The contraction of the core will then bring the shoulders around. Since the arms are out in front of the chest, they follow the shoulders around.

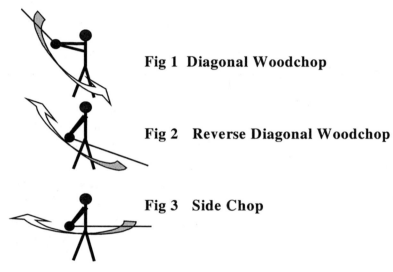

Fig 1 Diagonal Woodchop

Fig 2   Reverse Diagonal Woodchop

Fig 3   Side Chop

Try this routine for a month. You can use it to warm up for a round of golf, a tennis match, prior to a softball game, or any other sport which requires rotation. Establish your rotational strength and by the time you finish this 4-week program, you are ready to go ballistic!

"CORE training":
Training from the inside out!
PART III
By
Juan Carlos Santana, MEd., CSCS

Part I on core development took the beginning trainee and provided a very basic conditioning stimulus for the abdominal and lower back. Part II stood the individual up and the movements became more "functional" (i.e. simulating more "real life" movements). The standing position gets the legs involved in force generation. The proper synchronization of the legs and core is a very important aspect of functional power development, since any dissipation of energy between the source (i.e. ground) and the final target (i.e. ball) will result in decreased performance. One can have very strong individual body parts but if they are not coordinated properly in a move, the outcome will be less than favorable. A perfect example of this is Tiger Woods. Tiger is not as strong as other professional power athletes. However, he consistently out drives stronger athletes during celebrity golf tournaments. Even if you take away the technical aspect, which accounts for the accuracy portion of the game and just look at the raw mechanics of the club swing, it is Tiger's ability to synchronize his muscle movement that allows for his greater power output and longer drives!

This last section on core development takes us to our final objective, the conversion from strength to power. It is at this last stage where you will really start to notice real and significant improvements in your ability to quickly change directions and perform various sporting activities like swinging a golf club or tennis racket. If you have completed the beginning and intermediate routines laid out in our Part I and Part II of this series, you have laid down the proper strength foundation for the more demanding movements of power development. At this point, the focus will be to execute some of the movements we have already performed in Part II, however with two main differences.

First, the movements will become ballistic. This will teach the strong muscles you have developed to produce force in a rapid manner. Secondly, and most importantly, the element of "release" is added to the exercise. Most exercises used in strength training are performed in a "controlled" fashion. This means the implement you use (e.g. a barbell) is accelerated through a range of motion, then decelerated until it stops at the end of the movement. As much as 50% of the energy used in traditional strength training exercise is dedicated to the deceleration of the weight. This allocation of energy to deceleration hinders power development. Since throwing has no deceleration component, the ability to throw a heavy object allows power development through the full range of an activity.

Medicine balls are one of my favorite tools for developing functional power in athletes and non-athletes alike. Today's medicine balls are made very durable and can be thrown against walls. This next routine will really "transfer" all of that dynamic strength we have been developing with the two previous routines. It involves three different throws, which can be performed against any cement wall. An Overhead throw (Fig 1), a Side throw (to each side) (Fig 2) and a Back throw (Fig 3). Depending on the size and physical condition of the individual, a 1-3 kg medicine ball can be used. One can perform 3-5 sets of 6-8 repetitions for each throw, 2-3 times per week. Make sure you use your whole body when throwing the ball. Think of "conditioning yourself from your toe nails to finger nails". One should warm up thoroughly before attempting these explosive throws. Five minutes of dynamic warm-up exercises (e.g. 2-3 minutes of biking or jogging in place followed by 2-3 minutes of dynamic stretches) should get you ready for these throws. Following the warm-up, one set of the Stability ball exercises and one set of the band the exercises would enhance the warm up to the medicine ball throws.

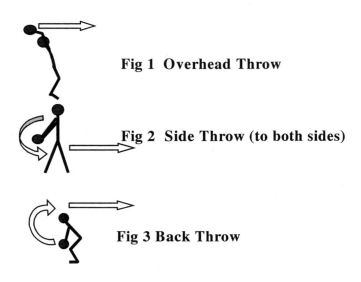

Fig 1 Overhead Throw

Fig 2 Side Throw (to both sides)

Fig 3 Back Throw

Go ahead and give this routine a try. Don't try to advance too quickly. Remember, going through the complete progression described in Part I and Part II of this series which will allow you time to develop proper core strength. This strength foundation is essential before advancing to the more explosive exercises in this program. It's common to have my tennis players, golfers, and baseball players notice considerable increases in their power within 2-3 weeks after starting this progression, along with their resistance training routine.

One point should be made in the closing of this article. The decelerators used in stopping the body and recovering after a throw, or a swinging of an implement, are also of prime importance. Many times these are muscles that are injured as a result in a strength imbalance between the body's accelerators and decelerators (e.g. the rear aspect of the shoulder is a common injury sight in throwers and tennis players). Correcting this imbalance will be addressed in future articles.

Suggested readings

1. Anderson GBJ, Bogduk N, Deluca C, et al; Muscle: Clinical perspectives on Low Back Pain. New Perspectives on Low Back Pain. Edited by JW Frymoyer, SL Gordon. Park Ridge, IL, American Academy of Orthopedic Surgeons, pp. 293-334, 1989.
2. Aosaki, T., et al. Responses of tonically active neurons in the primate's striatum undergo systematic changes during behavioral sensorimotor conditioning. J Neuroscience, 14(6): 3969-3984, 1994.
3. Boehme, Regi, OTR. Improving Upper Body Control. Tucson: Therapy Skill Builders, 1988.
4. Blievernicht, J. Balance: Course Manual. Chicago, IL 1996.
5. Brody, Liz. " The Axler: A Workout That's Really on the Ball." Shape. April 1993: 86-93.
6. Carrie, Beate, P.T. " Swiss Ball Exercises." PT Magazine. September; 92-100. 1993.
7. Carrie, Beate, P.T. and Linda Felix, P.T. " In Consideration of Proportions." PT Magazine. April 1993: 59.
8. Carter AT: Piriformis syndrome: A hidden cause of sciatic pain. Athl Training 1988; 23(3):243-245. 1975
9. Check P. Scientific Back Training: Correspondence Course Manual. Paul Chek Seminars. LaJolla, CA 1994.
10. Chek P. Scientific Abdominal Training. Correspondence Course Manual. Paul Chek Seminars. Lajolla, CA 1992.
11. Clark, M. "Focus on Function: Functional Anatomy Manual." The Athletic Institute. Tempe, Arizona, 1999.
12. Clark, M. "Foundations for Function". Learn by Doing Seminar Series, Coral Gables, Florida, 1999.
13. Cooper, Douglas. Dynamic Stabilization Exercises for the Lower Back. Portland: Douglas Cooper, 1992.
14. Creager, Caroline C. Theraputic Exercises Using the Swiss Ball. Boulder: Executive Physical Therapy, 1994.
15. Cresswell, A.G., Oddsson, L., Thorstensson, A. The influence of sudden perturbations on trunk muscle activity and intra-abdominal pressure while standing. Exp Brain Res, 98:336-341. 1994.
16. Dominguez, Richard H, MD, Gajada Robert. Total Body Training. New York: Warner Books, 1982.
17. Farfan HF. Effects of torsion on the intervertebral joints. Can J Surg 1969;12:336-341
18. Farfan HF. Musculature mechanism of the lumbar spine and the position of power and efficiency. Orthop Clin North Am 1975; 6:135-144
19. Farfan, H. F., Biomechanics of the Lumbar Spine in Managing Low Back Pain, Kirkaldy Willis, W.H., Ed. New York: Churchill-Livingston,1983.
20. Gambetta, V., Clark, M., " A formula for function", Training and Conditioning, 8(4):24-29, 1998.

21. Gambetta, V., Gary, G., "Following a functional path", Training and Conditioning, 5(2):25-30, 1995.
22. Gomez, Niska. Somarhythms: Developing Somatic Awareness with Large, Inflatable Balls." Somatics. Spring/Summer, 1992. Pp12-18.
23. Grabiner M. et al. Decoupling of bilateral paraspinal excitation in subjects with low back pain. Spine. 17(10):1219-1223. 1992.
24. Granhed H, Jonson R and Hansson T. The loads on the lumbar spine during extreme weight lifting. Spine. 12(2): 146-149. 1987
25. Gray, G.W., "Chain Reaction Festival," (Course Manual), Adrian, Michigan. Wynne Marketing.1996.
26. Headley BJ: The "Play-Ball" Exercise Program. St. Paul. Minnesota, Pain Resources, Ltd., 1990.
27. Hodges, P.W. , Richardson, C.A. Inefficient Muscular Stabilization of the Lumbar Spine Associated with Low Back Pain. Spine, 21(22):2640-2650, 1996.
28. Hodges, P.W., Richardson, C.A., Jull, G. Contraction of the Abdominal Muscles Associated with Movement of the Lower Limb. Phys Ther, 77:132-14, 1997.
29. Hypes, Barbara. Facilitating Development and Sensorimotor Function: Treatment with the Ball. Minnesota: P Press, 1991.
30. Klien-Vogelbach, Suzanne. Theraputic Exercises in Functional Kinetics. Germany: Springer-Velag, 1991.
31. Koes BW, Bouter LM, Beckerman H, et al. Physiotherapy exercises and back pain: a blinded review. BMJ. 1991; 302;1572-1576.
32. Kucera, Maria. Gymnastik mit dem Hupfball (Exercise with the GymBall). 5Th Edition. Stuttgart: Gustav Fischer Verlag, 1993.
33. Maurer, H. (no date) Gymnastik Ball. A Handout. 7112 Waldenburg zur Ausbildung von; Gymnastiklehrerinnen F.M.B.H.
34. Miller DJ: Comparison of electromyographic activity in the lumbar paraspinal muscles of subjects with and without chronic low back pain. Phys Ther 65:1347-1354, 1985.
35. Multiple Muscle Systems; Biomechanics and Movement Organization. Edited by Jack M. Winters and Savio L-Y Woo. pg 252-253
36. Nachemson A, Morris JM. In vivo measurements of intradiscal pressure. J Bone Joint Surg Am.;46:1077-1080. 1964
37. Nachemson AL: Disc Pressure measurements. Spine. 6;93-97, 1981.
38. Nachemson, A. The load on the lumbar disks in different positions of the body. Clin Orthop.;45:107-112. 1966
39. Nachemson, A.L., The Lumbar Spine, An Orthopedic Challenge. Spine 1:59, 1976.
40. Pace JB: Commonly overlooked pain syndromes responsive to simple therapy. Postgrad Med; 58(4):107-113.
41. Paruidge MJ, Walters CE. Participation of the abdominal muscles in various movements of the trunk in man, an EMG study. Physical Therapy Review;39;791-800. 1959
42. Porterfield J.A. and DeRosa C. Mechanical Low Back Pain. Philadelphia: W.B.Saunders Co. 1991
43. Posner-Mayer, J. Swiss Ball Applications for Orthopedic and Sports Medicine. Denver: Ball Dynamics International, Inc. 1995.

44. Rathke, F., Knupfer, H. (no date) Exercise Ball: Exercising tool for child development. A handout. Stutttgart. Municipal Center.

45. Robinson, R. The New Back School Prescription: Stabilization Training Part I. Occupt Med. 7(1):17-31. 1992.

46. Saal J. Dynamic Muscular stabilization in the Nonoperative treatment of lumbar pain syndromes, in Orthopedic Review Vol. XlX No. 8 Aug 1990.

47. Saal J. et al. Non operative management of herniated cervical intervertebral disc with radiculopathy. Spine,. 21(16). 1996

48. Santana, JC. The Essence of Stability Ball Training, Vol I-II. Optimum Performance Systems, Boca Raton, Florida, 1999.

49. Seroussi RE, Pope MH: The relationship between trunk muscle electromyography and lifting moments in the sagittal and frontal planes. J. Biomech . 20: 135-146, 1987.

50. Sieg, K., Adams, S. Illustrated Essentials of Musculoskeletal Anatomy. Gainsville, Fl. Megabooks, Inc. 1985.

51. Sweet, Waldo E. Sport and Recreation in Ancient Greece: A sourcebook with Translations. New York: Oxford University Press, 1987.

52. Wirhed, R. Athletic ability and the anatomy of motion. Wolf Medical Publications. 1990.

53. Wolpaw, J.R., Braitmman, D. J., Seegal. Adaptive plasticity in the primate spinal reflex: initital development. J Neurophysiology. 50:1296-1311, 1983.

54. Wolpaw, J.R. Acquisition and maintenance of the simplest motor skill: investigation of CNS. Med. Sci. Sports Exerc. 26(12):1475-1479, 1994.

55. Zetterberg C, Andersson GBJ, Schultz AB: The activity of individual trunk muscles during heavy physical loading. Spine 12:1035-1040, 1987.

For more information on the OPS seminar series and consulting, call:

Optimum Performance Systems

438 NW 13 St
Boca Raton, Florida 33432
(561) 393-3881

email - jcs@opsfit.com
Web Page - www.opsfit.com

DONAHUE